Guide for Expectant Parents

Guide for

EXPECTANT PARENTS

by

Maternity Center Association

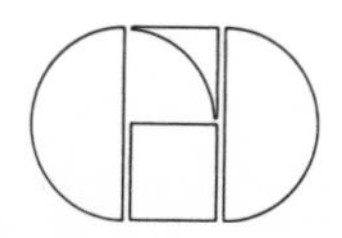

GROSSET & DUNLAP

Publishers / New York

Published Simultaneously in Canada

Library of Congress Catalog Card Number: 70-78054

Portions of this book previously
appeared in *Baby Care Manual,* November, 1968.

Printed in the United States of America

Contents

Introduction

by

R. Gordon Douglas, M.D.

Dr. Douglas is a distinguished obstetrician and gynecologist. He was formerly Chairman of the Medical Board of Maternity Center Association and professor of Obstetrics and Gynecology at Cornell University Medical College, and is a past president of the American College of Obstetricians and Gynecologists.

This is a handbook for expectant mothers and fathers, written by the professional staff of the Maternity Center Association. It is full of helpful hints, practical suggestions and illustrations. It is a book to be read through to get the "feel" of what happens during pregnancy, birth and afterwards. But its chief purpose is to be "on hand" to answer questions as they arise during the important days and months in the life of an unborn baby and his mother and father. The reader will find a complete index at the end of the book.

Maternity Center Association is a national organization which has been working for better maternity care for fifty years. Its staff has listened to and answered questions of expectant parents in classes, in clinics and in private consultations. The one hundred questions in this book are among those most frequently asked at Maternity Center. The answers are straightforward and reassuring, such as might be given by a doctor or nurse to a questioning patient.

We hope that this little book will answer the readers' questions. But remember, nothing takes the place of signing up with a doctor (or a maternity clinic) just as soon as pregnancy is suspected–*and then going back regularly, as suggested.*

May this book help to make pregnancy a healthful and happy time for you.

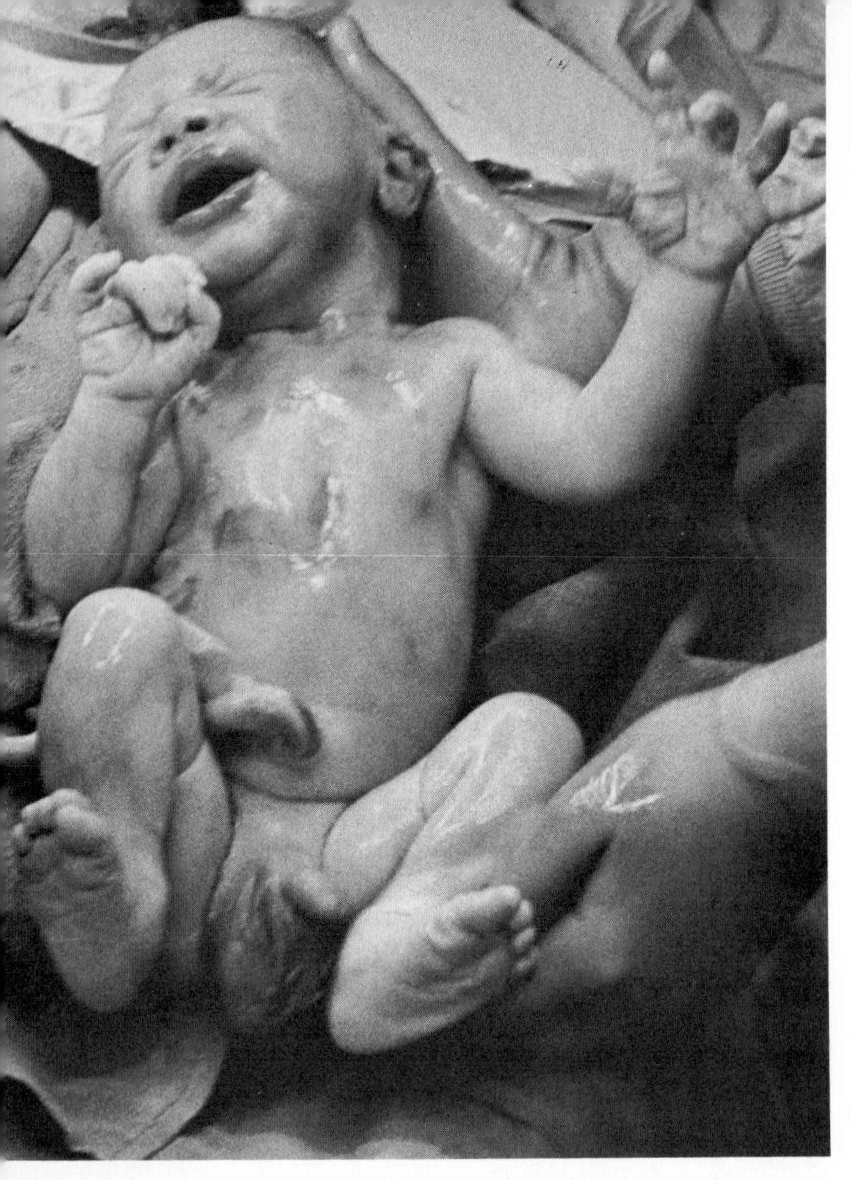

Fig. 1 Just after birth. *Photo by Bob Cacace*

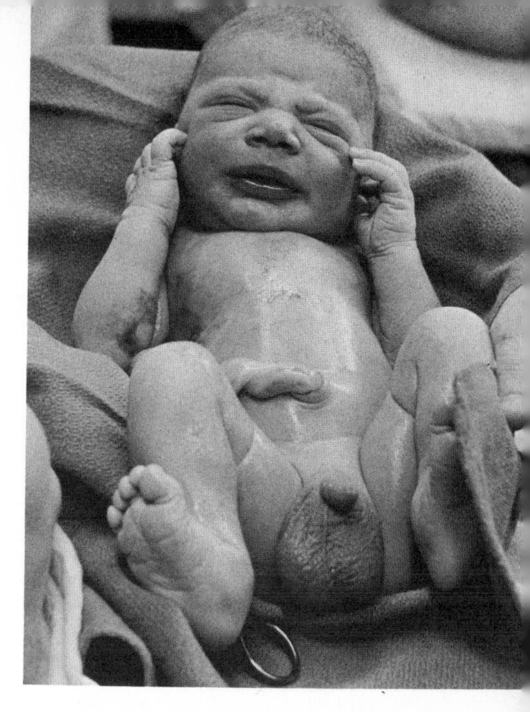

Fig. 2 The baby's umbilical cord is not yet cut. *Photo by Bob Cacace*

I

About the Baby

1. WHAT IS A NEWBORN BABY LIKE?

The picture on these and the next two pages were taken right after birth (Figs. 1–5). Newborn babies do not have that pink-and-blue-ribbon look that you see in the magazines. But they win your heart with their own special charm.

Now let's take a look at a newborn baby from head to toe:

Face: A newborn baby's face is usually round and full, with a receding chin (Fig. 6).

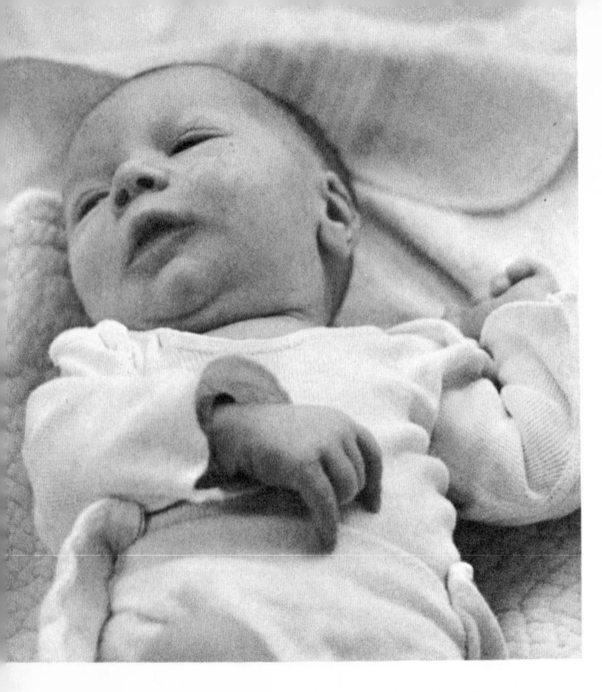

Fig. 3 Same baby all tidied up—an hour after birth. *Photo by Bob Cacace*

Fig. 4 Safe beside mother. *Photo by Maria LaYacona*

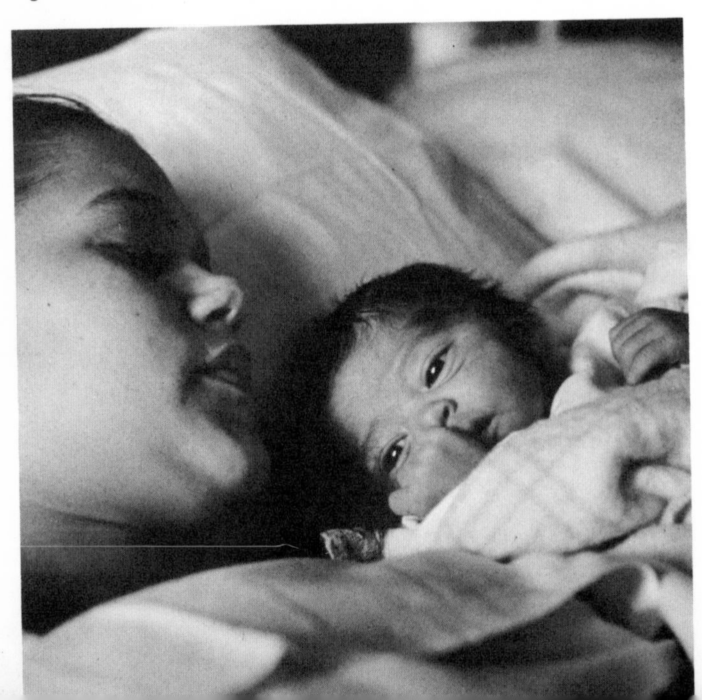

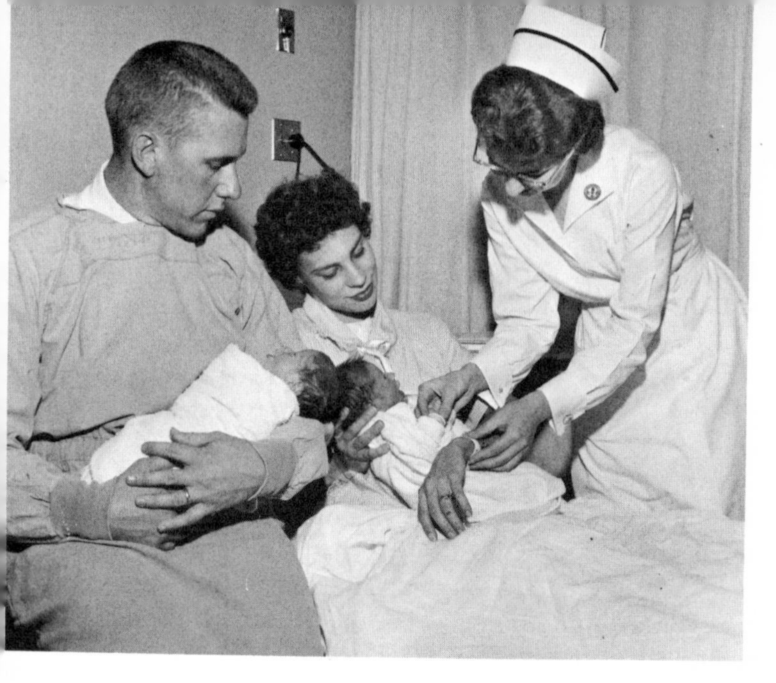

Fig. 5 Double-take.

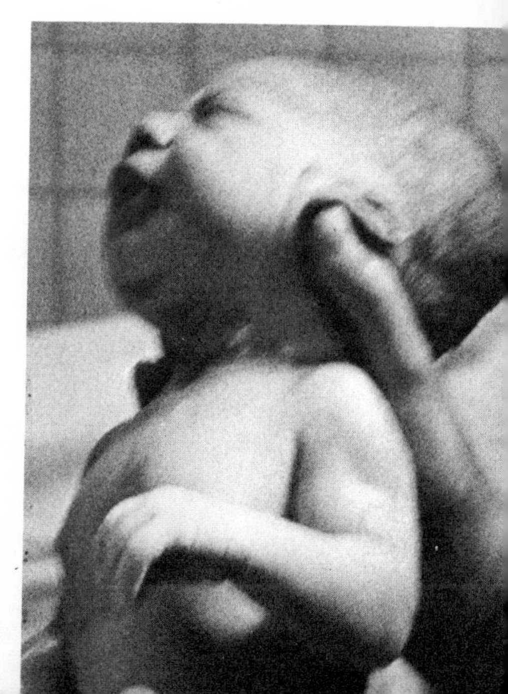

Fig. 6 Round face—receding chin and molded head. *Photo by Bob Cacace*

Arms, legs and trunk: His arms and trunk are well rounded, but his legs are less finished in appearance and thin in comparison with the rest of his body. He may look bowlegged. His chest is like a barrel, and his abdomen sticks out (Fig. 7).

Vernix: If the pictures were in color, you would see more clearly the vernix, which covers the skin or may be just in the creases. Vernix, which looks like cold cream, used to be washed off before a baby was brought to his parents for introduction. But now, because it is known that vernix protects the skin from infection and irritation, he usually doesn't get a bath for the first few days.

Skin: When you take off his clothes or change his diaper, you may discover that his skin is blotchy. This is natural for a newborn baby.

Before-birth position: At first, the baby may lie in the same position he had in the uterus (womb). His back is rounded and his legs drawn up. It may take several days before he relaxes and straightens out.

Raising his head: The newborn baby is often able to raise his head while lying on his tummy.

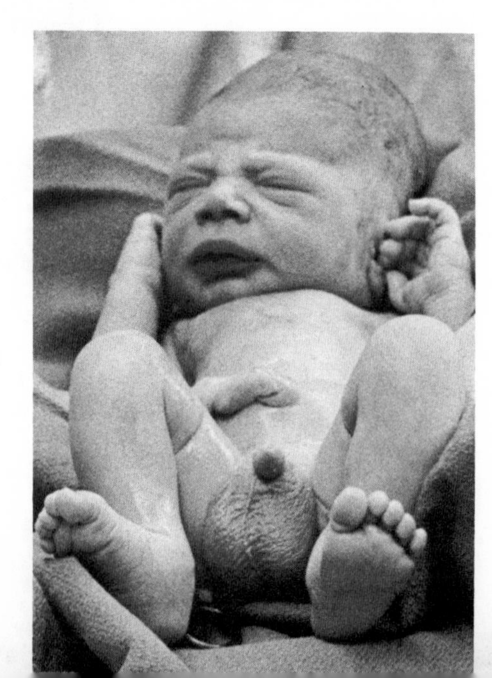

Fig. 7 Barrel-chested boy. *Photo by Bob Cacace*

Learning to breathe: At first, the baby's breaths may be irregular and shallow. Sometimes they are so quiet that you can't hear them, and sometimes so noisy that he may wake you up in the middle of the night.

Hiccups: He may get hiccups, and his lower jaw may quiver. This is natural, too.

Fast heart rate: A baby's heart beats much faster than an adult's before he is born, and this continues for some time after birth. It may beat 130 to 140 times a minute —and when he is crying, it may go up to 180.

Early loss of weight: Expect the baby to lose almost one-tenth of his birth weight in the first five days of life. When he is born, his body contains much extra water which he loses rapidly. After about the fifth day, he will begin to gain; and by the tenth day, he has usually regained his birth weight. But don't be surprised if your baby does not gain so fast: each baby has his own rate of growth.

How big is a baby? Size depends on a number of things, such as the size of his parents and grandparents; whether he arrives at the end of nine months or before; or how well fed he is. Most newborn babies are around seven pounds and are about twenty inches long.

Baby hair: Some babies are born with a full head of hair; others with little or none. The new-baby hair gradually wears away, and then permanent hair comes in. This may be a different color. And the little fellow born with no hair may grow the thickest thatch of curls you ever saw.

Size and shape of baby's head: A newborn baby's head is big in comparison with the rest of his body— about one quarter of his body length. All of the bones are soft and pliable; so his head is shaped to fit the birth canal while he is being born (see Fig. 6). Soon the head takes on the familiar roundness of babyhood.

Sight: Before birth, the baby's eyes develop earlier and more fully than other parts of his body. At birth, the eyes are three quarters the adult size. A new baby cannot see clearly, but he can tell light from dark. The eyes of the fair-skinned are usually blue-gray; of the dark-skinned, brown. Sometimes one eye may be a darker shade than the other. In a few weeks, the baby's eyes take on their permanent coloring. Sometimes the eyes appear slightly crossed (Fig. 8), but they usually straighten out within a few months.

Touch: The sense of touch is still undeveloped in the newborn baby's fingertips, so he explores his world with the palms of his hands.

Taste: Taste is the baby's best-developed sense. He reacts to sweet, sour, bitter and salty tastes.

Hearing: The baby can hear, and he responds to loud sounds with quick, jumpy movements. It is known that a baby, even in his mother's uterus, responds to vibrations. One mother reported to her doctor that her un-

Fig. 8 Eyes may be slightly crossed. *Photo by Bob Cacace*

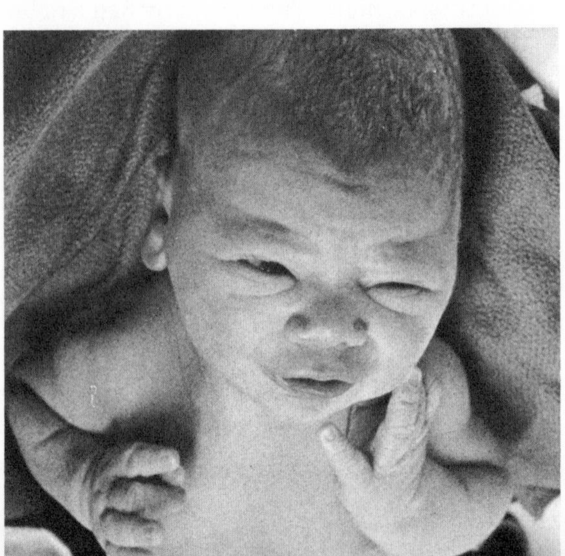

born child became troublesomely active whenever she went to a concert during the later weeks of pregnancy. Another noticed that the baby jumped in her womb whenever she came within range of the humming of her washing machine. Another found that when she knocked on her bathtub while bathing, the baby seemed startled.

During the time when the baby is in the uterus, he is surrounded by the steady "throb-throb" of his mother's heartbeat. When he is born, it is thought by some that he may miss this familiar sound. If he becomes quiet when held against his mother's breast, perhaps it is the steady throbbing of her heart that gives him comfort.

Sucking reflex: The baby sucks his thumb long before he is born. So, at birth, his sucking reflex is ready. The slightest touch on his lip causes him to suck. He is ready and able to take his food.

Sleep: A baby sleeps most of the time. But his sleep is lighter than an older child's. His eyelids flutter. His eyes roll around. His mouth twitches. He may smile. Because there was no day or night inside his mother, the baby may at first sleep in the day and be wakeful at night. He will gradually get used to day and night, but at first you'll have to accept these sleeping-waking periods as they occur. You'll notice how expertly he can stretch, screw up his face and yawn.

Baby needs love: The experience of being outside the womb is new to the baby. He likes to be held and loved. He likes to feel the warmth of his mother's body. He likes to be rocked and to hear his mother talking to him and humming. He likes to be fed and to have a chance to suck. He quickly learns when he is being held by his mother. He knows her through his sense of smell, taste and touch; he recognizes the sound of her voice.

All this tells him he is being mothered, and it is very important to him.

Crying: A baby has to cry. He needs the exercise. It is also a way of talking to you. He cries when he is wet or soiled, too hot or too cold, or just hungry. Your tender, loving care will help him over these uncomfortable moments. It is not always easy for you, but it can be rewarding. For instance, you hold your little one on your shoulder because he is squirming and shrieking. What *can* be the matter? Suddenly he gives a big b-u-r-p and quickly settles down to blissful peace and quiet.

No average baby: There isn't any such thing as an average baby or, for that matter, an average child or adult—except in statistics. Charts and guide books are based on the records of thousands of babies, but no one baby fits the picture. Your baby may be smaller than you expected—bigger—redder—prettier—noisier. He may smile, talk or walk days before or after the so-called average. Try to enjoy him for himself.

When the baby is ready (Fig. 9), he comes out of the "escape hatch" (the cervix and birth canal) by the process called labor (see Questions 47 to 67). When he is born, he has feelings and emotions, so he needs to feel loved and wanted.

Fig. 9 The baby comes out of the 'escape hatch,' the birth canal, and is born.

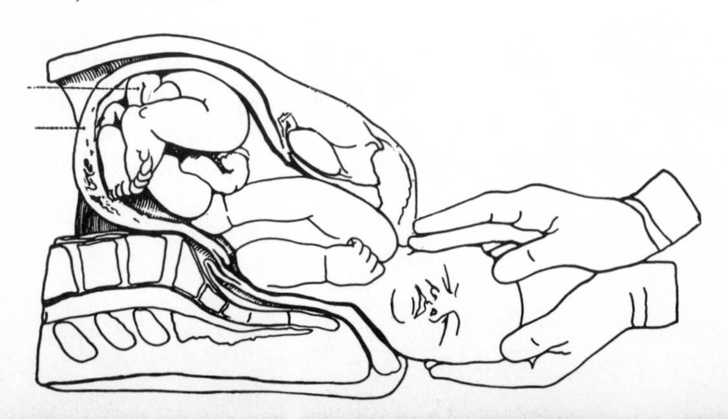

2. HOW DOES THE BABY LIVE AND GROW BEFORE HE IS BORN?

One of the most important periods in the baby's life is the time he spends in quiet, steady growth in his mother's uterus. He grows more rapidly at that time than he ever will again: from a tiny fertilized ovum—not even the size of this dot · —to a complete baby.

How can this happen in the short space of nine months? Science is only beginning to find some of the answers. The beginning of life is still the greatest mystery of the universe. What is known, however, is thrilling. Knowing something about the baby's development may help you to appreciate him better when you hold him for the first time.

Baby and Astronaut

Each of us has lived in a capsule (the uterus) for nine months—with some of the same conditions that astronauts live in when they orbit the earth. Space scientists are only beginning to catch up with the engineering design of the human uterus. Nature developed the uterus—perhaps billions of years ago—to protect the unborn baby. It is built to:

control VIBRATION
provide FOOD and OXYGEN

Fig. 10 Human space capsule. Similarity between uterus and astronaut in outer space capsule.

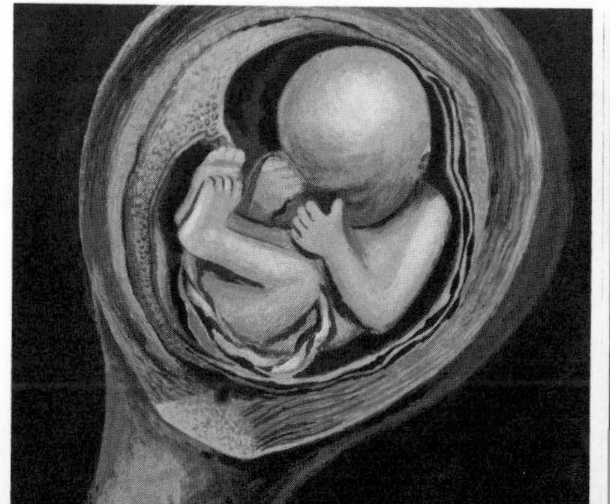

protect against SUDDEN PRESSURE CHANGES
control WEIGHTLESSNESS,
TEMPERATURE and the
PULL OF GRAVITY

The capsule used for outer space is shaped like the human uterus (Fig. 10). It, too, has an escape hatch at the lower end to release the astronaut when he is ready to go outside.

Living Under Water

In early research of space science, it was found that test animals could stand rapid speed-ups much better if they were under water and didn't have to get necessary oxygen by breathing air. Nature worked this out thousands of centuries ago for the baby in the uterus. The baby lives completely submerged in water and protected against the damaging effects of even 1G (normal gravity) on his delicate tissues.

Floating in a sac of water also protects the baby from stress and strain of vibration and sudden jars and jolts. The water keeps him at an even temperature—the best for his developing body and brain. The water lets the baby move about freely without the pull of gravity, as the mother will notice when he begins to exercise his arms and legs. The baby, floating in fluid (like the skin diver), may have some of the feelings of weightlessness felt by the astronaut who circles the earth at 18,000 miles an hour.

Need for Oxygen

The astronaut and the unborn baby must get enough oxygen; neither can live long without it. One of the problems of the space scientist is how to provide enough oxygen for long trips—say, to the moon and back. The baby gets his oxygen from his mother's bloodstream through the placenta (afterbirth). She breathes in the air. The oxygen in the air is carried by her blood to the placenta. From there it goes into the baby's bloodstream (see Question 8). The baby's heart then pumps his blood containing the oxygen to every part of his body.

The baby in the uterine capsule has an advantage over the astronaut because the baby can live in an atmosphere equal to the rarefied air seven miles above the earth's surface. He can do this because he has more and larger oxygen-carrying red blood cells than adults have. Also, the baby's brain at this time does not need as much oxygen in order to grow and function.

Waste Disposal

The disposal of body wastes is another challenge to space scientists. For the baby, however, nature long ago solved this problem. The waste products of the baby's body chemistry are absorbed by the mother's bloodstream through the placenta and disposed of through her kidneys and lungs (Fig. 11).

Fig. 11 The placenta or afterbirth is a temporary organ which carries food and oxygen, minerals and hormones to the growing baby, and transfers the baby's waste products to the mother's bloodstream for disposal by her kidneys and lungs.

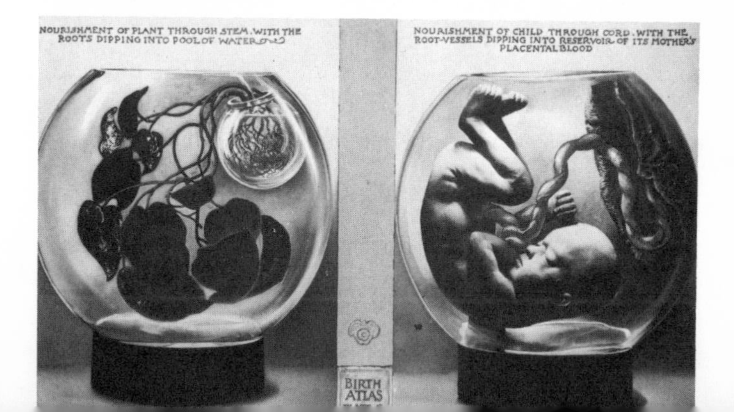

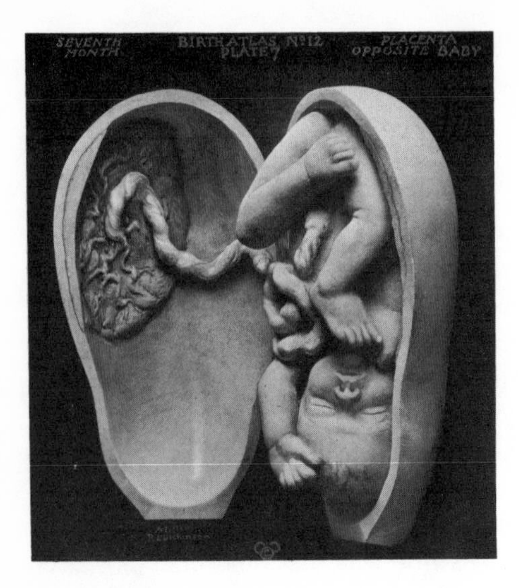

Fig. 12 Seventh month: placenta opposite baby.

3. WHAT HAPPENS TO THE BABY DURING PREGNANCY?

Months in a Capsule

Baby at 28 Weeks (Fig. 12)

The baby weighs about two pounds. He looks well developed, but at this age he is far from ready for birth. If born now, he would find life on the outside troublesome. His breathing would be difficult. His temperature-regulating apparatus is not finished, so he would have to be kept in an incubator. He would have to be fed very carefully and handled by nurses specially trained in the care of premature babies. Some very young premature babies do manage to make this adjustment to life. While they may be more difficult to raise in the early months, many gradually catch up with full-term babies who were born about the same time.

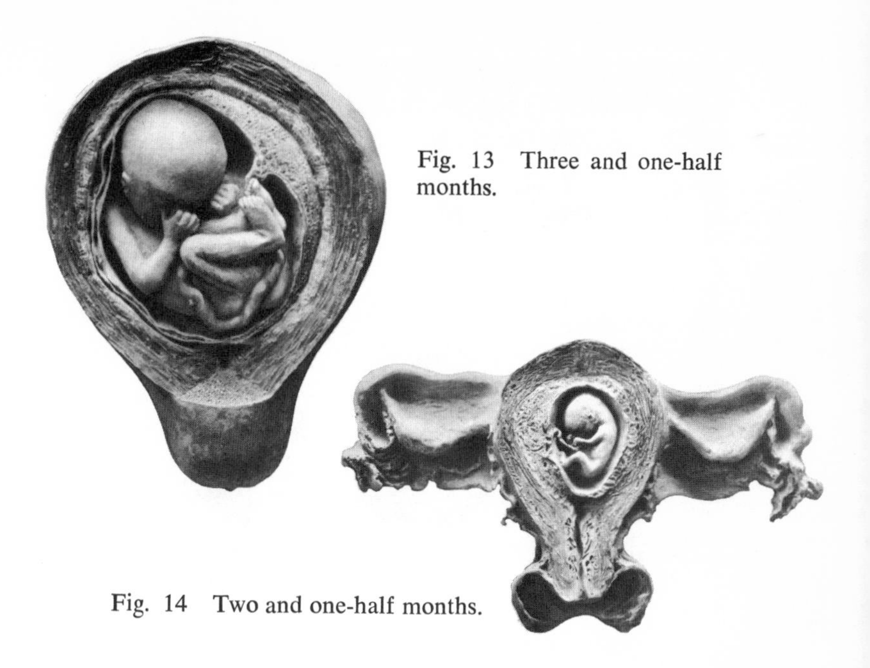

Fig. 13 Three and one-half months.

Fig. 14 Two and one-half months.

Baby at 14 Weeks (Fig. 13)

He looks like a miniature baby—only about four inches long—with short arms and legs. His fingers and toes are exquisitely formed. His nails are beginning to grow. Baby teeth are well started in his gums.

Baby at 10 Weeks (Fig. 14)

At this very early age—just a few weeks after the mother suspects that she is pregnant—the baby has the beginnings of all his organs. He has eyes, nose and mouth, fingers and toes. Bones are beginning to harden, muscles to form. The baby can move. His head has grown more rapidly than the rest of his body, so it looks a bit out of proportion.

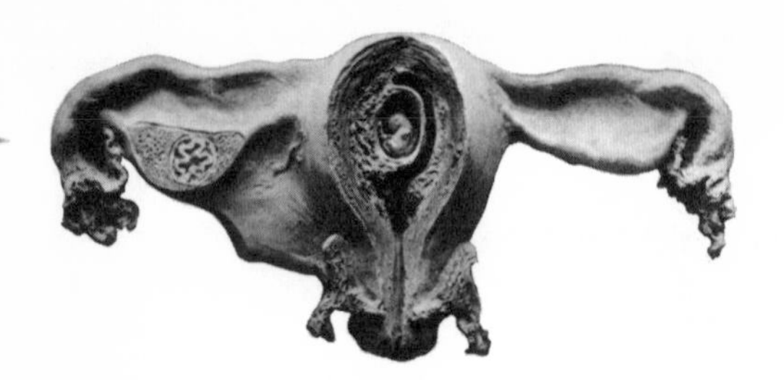

Fig. 15 Seven weeks.

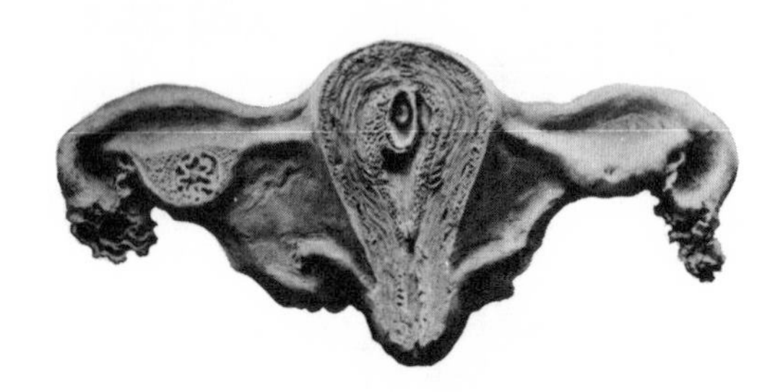

Fig. 16 Six weeks.

Baby at 7 Weeks (Fig. 15)

From the baby's tiny body—less than an inch long—buds are growing that will soon be arms and legs. His lifeline is the umbilical cord containing the blood vessels that carry his blood to and from the developing placenta.

Baby at 6 Weeks (Fig. 16)

By the time the mother's first menstrual period is missed, the baby's body is well started. He has buds for eyes, ears, sex organs; and his backbone is forming. His heart muscle has been beating for some time.

4. WHERE DOES THE BABY'S LIFE BEGIN?

The baby's life begins deep in the mother's body in the tube, leading to her womb, which is protected by the bony cradle of the pelvis (Fig. 17).

The uterus (womb) is a hollow organ measuring about 3-by-2-by-1 inches. By the end of pregnancy, it measures about 12-by-9-by-8 inches. Its capacity has increased five hundred times! In weight it grows from about one-and-one-half ounces to about thirty ounces (Fig. 18).

The muscle fibers that make up the uterus grow to ten times their original length and five times their original thickness. After the baby is born, the uterus returns to about the same size as before pregnancy.

At the top of the uterus on the left and right are two tubes, called *oviducts* or Fallopian tubes, leading to the *ovaries*. The ovaries are about the shape and size

Fig. 17 The uterus is protected by the bony cradle of the pelvis. The wide-flaring bones are the hip bones. The circle below the uterus is the opening through which the baby is born.

of big almonds. In the ovaries are thousands of ova, or eggs. About once a month one of these ova becomes ripe and bursts out of the ovary (Fig. 19). It is snatched up by the fringed ends of the oviduct (Fig. 20) and begins its journey down this tube to the uterus in expectation of meeting a male cell (sperm) on the way (Fig. 21).

Fig. 18 The uterus (A), Fallopian Tubes or oviducts (B), and the ovaries (C).

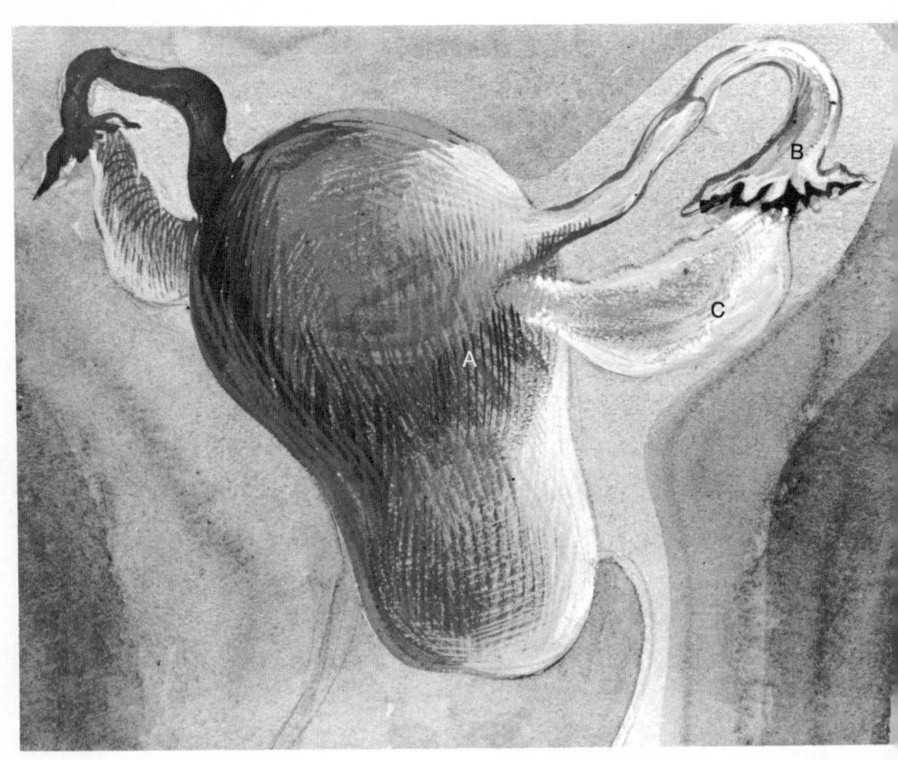

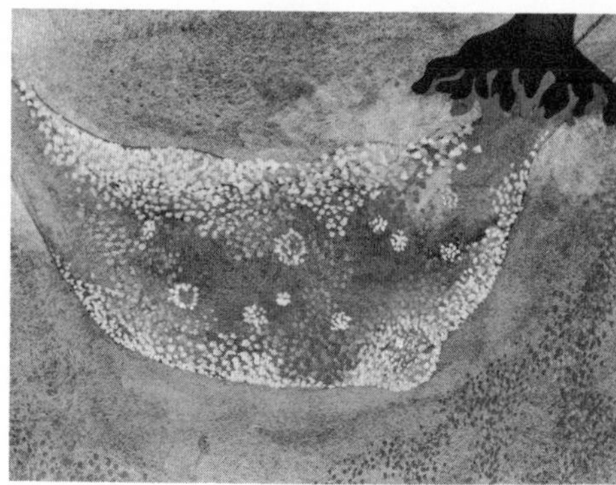

Fig. 19 At the lower part of the ovary, a ripe ovum is about to be released. This is called ovulation.

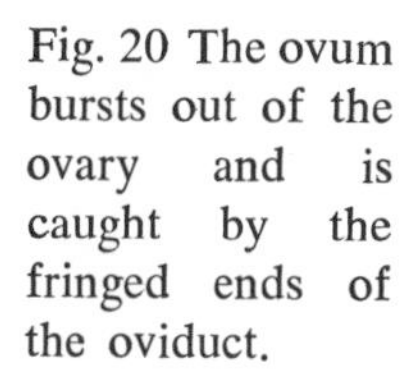

Fig. 20 The ovum bursts out of the ovary and is caught by the fringed ends of the oviduct.

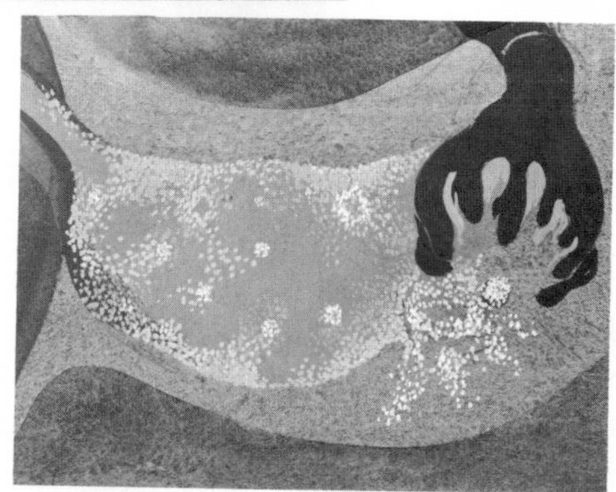

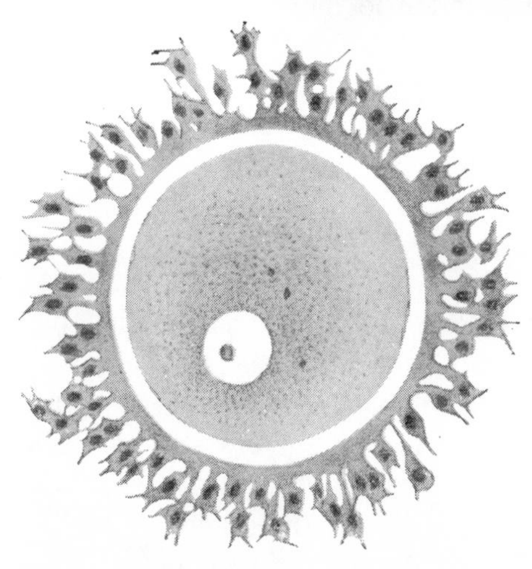

Fig. 21 The ovum—about the size of a tiny grain of sand—can barely be seen by the unaided human eye. It is covered with hundreds of 'nurse cells' which provide energy and building materials for its journey down the oviduct. Beneath these 'nurse cells' is a tough clear membrane. Inside is a liquid which contains the nucleus. Here are the genes and chromosomes carrying the baby's inheritance from his mother's side of the family. If the ovum is not fertilized by the cell (sperm) of a man within 24 hours after it leaves the ovary, it shrinks and passes from the woman's body in her secretion.

Fig. 22 (Left) The sperm is much smaller than the ovum—so small that it can be seen only under a powerful microscope. The head, midpiece and tail are designed to do four things: (1) The sperm must swim to the ovum. It gets this energy from the midpiece which drives the whiplike tail. (2) The sperm must find the ovum, usually in the oviduct. (3) It must break through the outer covering of the ovum. (4) It fertilizes the ovum, bringing to it the genes and chromosomes from the father's side of the family. These are contained in the nucleus (in its head). *Drawing by Frank Robinson.*

5. HOW DOES THE BABY'S LIFE BEGIN?

In the moment of sexual and emotional union of a man and woman, as many as four hundred million tiny sperm (Fig. 22) are deposited in the woman's vagina, which is the passageway leading to the uterus.

The sperm swim upward through the vagina, the uterus and into both oviducts. If an ovum is in one of the oviducts, the sperm quickly surround it—millions of them pushing, struggling to get inside (Figs. 23 and 24). The sperm move their tails in rhythm, often turning the ovum round and round for as long as twenty to thirty hours. They contain in their heads a chemical which dissolves the outer wall of the ovum. It used to be thought that only one sperm could enter the ovum. But now it is known that, while a number may get inside, only one can fertilize the ovum.

Genes and Chromosomes

In the head of the sperm is a tiny spot, called the nucleus, which has in it all the traits that the baby will inherit from his father's side of the family. The ovum has a matching nucleus with traits from the mother's side of the family.

Inside each nucleus are twenty-three smaller bodies called chromosomes. The chromosomes contain thousands of genes. Each one of these genes carries a single

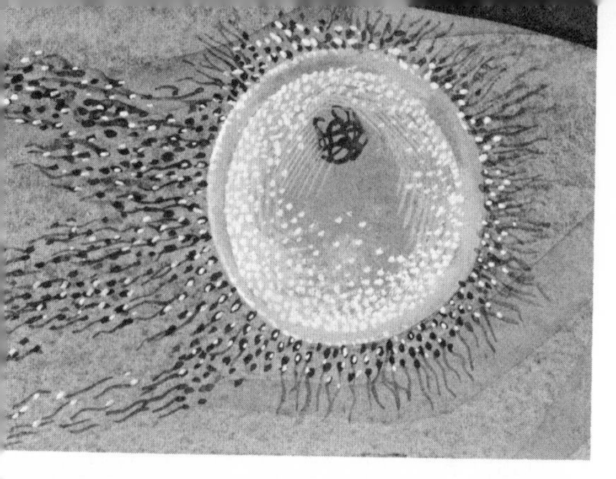

Fig. 23 Millions of sperm surround the ovum. Each carries in its head a chemical which dissolves the outer membrane of the ovum.

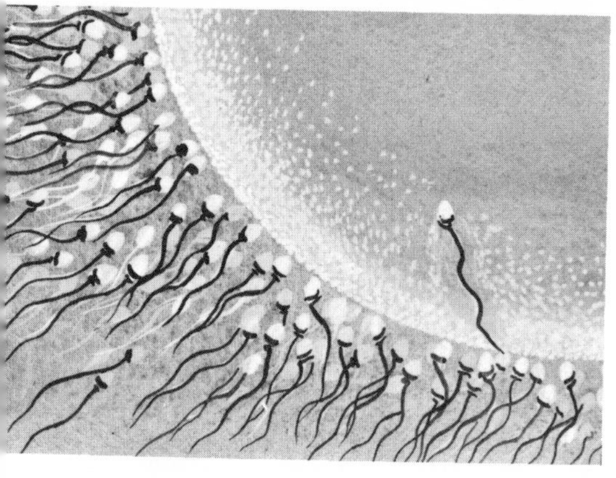

Fig. 24 At last one is successful. This is the moment of the beginning of a new person!

trait for: color of eyes, color of hair, shape of face, shape of nose, curve of lips, length of fingers and toes, etc.

Human sperm normally live about a day, and reach the oviduct in less than an hour after intercourse. The meeting of sperm and ovum usually takes place in the outer third of the oviduct. Once inside the ovum, the whiplash of the sperm's tail slows down. But, in a peculiar jumping motion, the sperm moves forward until its head, bearing the male nucleus, is close to the female nucleus in the ovum. The two nuclei approach, meet and unite. The joining of the twenty-three chromosomes in the male nucleus and the twenty-three chromosomes in the female nucleus gives life to a new person with forty-six chromosomes (Figs. 25A, 25B, 25C, 25D).

The baby's life has begun. The fertilized ovum begins to divide. The two-cell stage is reached after about thirty hours. As the fertilized ovum continues its journey down the oviduct, it develops into a cluster of cells (Fig. 26).

When it completes its journey down the oviduct, it settles on the wall of the uterus which is made ready once a month with an enriched supply of blood to feed the fertilized ovum. The outer cells of the fertilized ovum dissolve the surrounding tissue, and the lining of the uterus closes over it.

This is the baby's snug home for the next nine months.

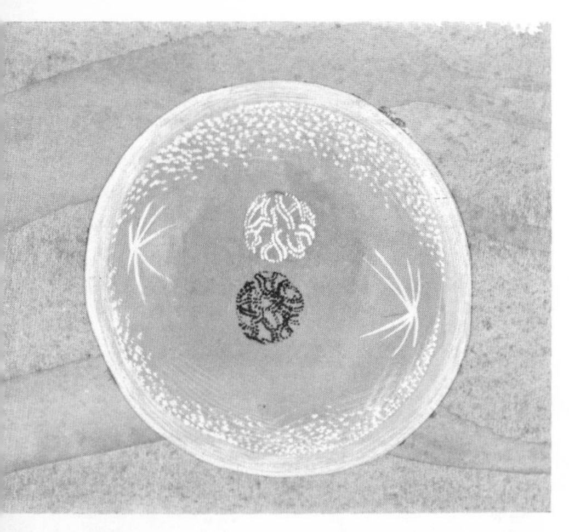

Fig. 25A The nuclei of the ovum and sperm approach each other inside the ovum.

Fig. 25B The genes and chromosomes from mother and father intermingle and unite.

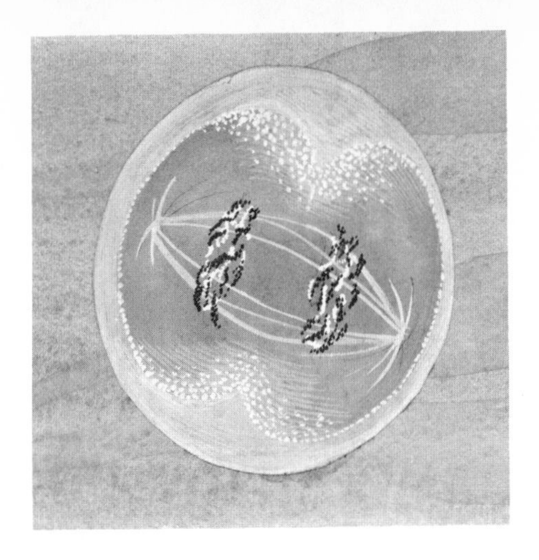

Fig. 25C The halves are drawn to opposite poles on spidery spindles.

Fig. 25D Two new cells are formed with equal numbers of chromosomes from mother and father.

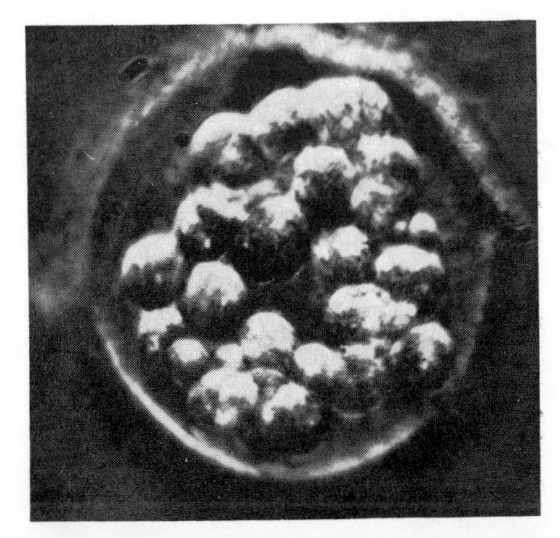

Fig. 26 As the fertilized ovum continues its journey down the oviduct, the cells multiply. This is a microphotograph of the cell cluster just before it reaches the uterus and is ready to settle down for its nine-month growth period before birth.

Microphotograph by Dr. Landrum B. Shettles

6. WILL IT BE A BOY OR A GIRL?

Nobody has as yet worked out a practical test to tell whether a baby in the uterus is a boy or a girl. Maybe it is good that we can't tell.

The Shah of Iran, a number of years ago, divorced his Queen because it was announced that she could not bear him male children. This was pure male arrogance, for science has known for a long time that the female ovum plays no part in the determination of sex.

About half of the father's sperm carry male-producing chromosomes. The other half contain female-producing chromosomes. So the father and pure chance determine the sex of the baby.

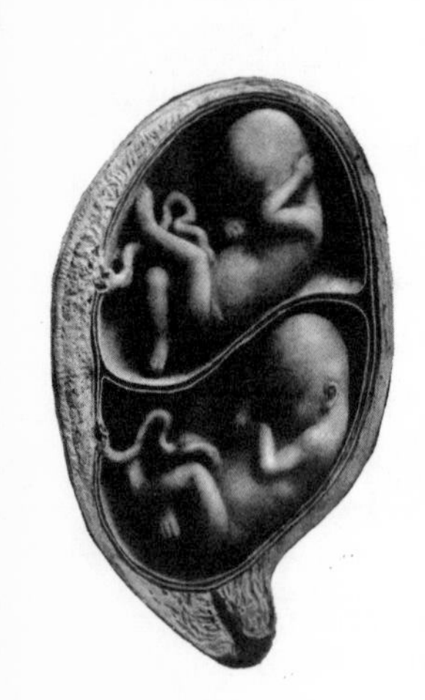

Fig. 27 (Left) Identical or one-egg twins. They developed from one ovum, fertilized by one sperm. Both babies are in a single outer sac but each has its own inner membrane. They share the same placenta. Identical twins are always the same sex and look alike.

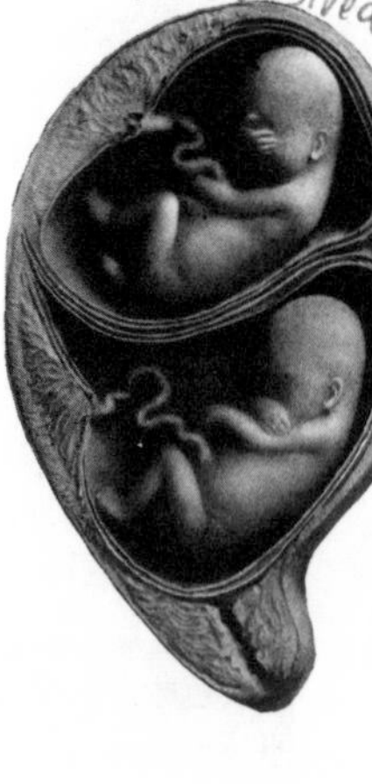

Fig. 28 (Right) Fraternal or two-egg twins. They developed from two separate ova, fertilized by two separate sperm. Each twin has his own double-membrane sac and placenta. Sex of fraternal twins can be different.

7. WILL IT BE TWINS?

There are two kinds of twins, triplets . . . sextuplets. One set comes from the division of the same fertilized ovum into a number of babies. Each baby is of the same sex and is the image of the others. They all are nurtured by the same placenta (afterbirth) and live in the same double-membrane sac (bag of waters) (Fig. 27).

The other set comes from several ova being fertilized by several sperm within the same general time. These babies can be of different sexes and may not look any more alike than other brothers and sisters. Each of these babies has its own placenta and its own sac of water (Fig. 28).

Sometimes one baby has a better blood supply than the other and may grow bigger and stronger in the uterus. Usually twins are smaller than single babies. Triplets, quadruplets and quintuplets are even smaller, because the uterus can grow only so big. The smaller babies often need special care, just like "preemies" (premature babies).

8. WHAT IS THE PLACENTA (AFTERBIRTH) AND WHAT DOES IT DO FOR THE BABY?

The baby gets his oxygen, food, hormones, minerals and water through his mother's blood. Nature has provided an efficient filter between her bloodstream and the baby's, called the placenta. This is a temporary organ which develops mainly from the lining of the uterus when the baby first settles into it.

The baby's heart pumps his blood to and from the placenta by way of blood vessels in the umbilical cord. If we could look inside the cord, we would see three blood vessels—one large vein carrying blood with oxygen and food to the baby and two smaller arteries carrying blood with waste products from the baby to the placenta. These three vessels are encased in a pale blue-green gelatinous substance. The whole cord is covered by a thin shining membrane.

The baby's bloodstream adjoins the mother's bloodstream in the placenta, but the two never meet (Fig. 29). The food and oxygen from the mother and the waste materials from the baby pass through a thin cellular wall which acts as a filter, often keeping germs and other harmful chemicals from the baby.

In this way, the baby is able to live and grow without breathing while he is in the uterus. After he is born, the placenta is also expelled—which is why it is sometimes called the afterbirth.

If a brother or sister comes along, another placenta grows to meet the new baby's needs.

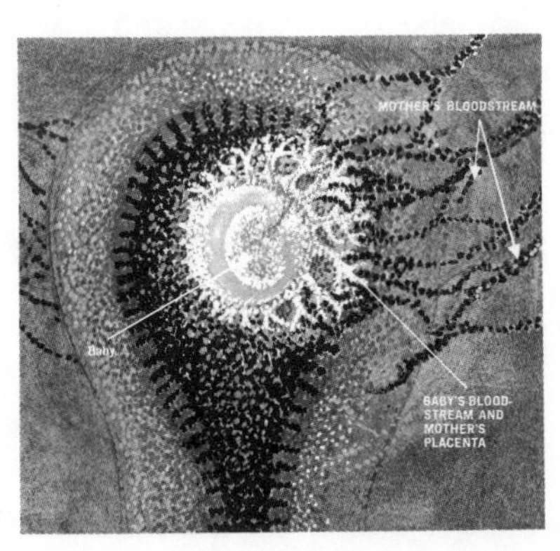

Fig. 29 In the placenta, mother's and baby's bloodstreams never meet. The food (from the mother) and waste products (from the baby) pass through a thin wall of cells.

9. HOW TO FIGURE OUT THE BABY'S BIRTHDAY?

What was the date of the beginning of your last menstrual period? Add seven days and count back three months. Example: *Last menstrual period began on January 1st. Add seven days—to the 8th of January. Count back three months. Expected date: next October 8th.* But don't count on it. The baby can come early or late.

II

About Pregnancy

In Early Pregnancy

10. HOW CAN A WOMAN KNOW THAT SHE IS PREGNANT? WHAT ARE THE SIGNS?

(a) Menstrual periods usually stop.

(b) In the early weeks, breasts may tingle. The circle around the nipples becomes darker. The blood vessels within the breasts gradually become more visible through the skin.

(c) A pregnant woman may have some changes in

appetite and temperament. Yes, those cravings you've heard about can be real. Recently, on a radio program of the BBC in England, a doctor invited his listeners to write him if they had food cravings in early pregnancy. He received a deluge of letters. The women said that these food cravings seemed very important at the moment. Later they were amused at their behavior. Some women reported that they felt such shame about their cravings that they went to great lengths to keep them secret even from their husbands.

(d) Pregnancy can also affect a woman's sexual desires. Some enjoy sexual intercourse more during pregnancy, while others may not enjoy it at all. But a woman may have an even greater need for love and affection with this temporary decrease in sexual desire. Many women are shy about discussing intercourse with their husbands. This can cause needless brooding and unhappiness.

(e) About half of the mothers of first babies have some symptoms of nausea or upset stomach in the morning when they first get out of bed. The exact reason for this has been debated for years. Some experts seem to feel that it is caused by our way of life: that is, people just *expect* a mother to be sick. Among primitive people who do not expect nausea, very few, if any, of the women have morning sickness.

Several researchers have found that the women who reported morning sickness also said that all through their lives their digestive systems were upset by things that went wrong at home or at school or at work. In other words, *any* crisis or change of conditions made them sick or uncomfortable.

Of course, not all morning sickness is emotionally or culturally caused. It may have some other basis, such as changes in body chemistry. A mother should talk to her doctor if she has morning sickness. He may give her drugs that will calm her queasy stomach. A simple, old-fashioned remedy is to eat something dry and starchy—like crackers—before getting out of bed.

(f) In the early months of pregnancy, women are likely to urinate many more times than usual—often at night. This is caused by slight pressures of the enlarging uterus on the bladder.

(g) Toward the end of the fifth month, the mother feels the baby begin to move. This has been described as the "fluttering of a bird in a closed hand."

11. WHY DO THE MONTHLY PERIODS STOP DURING PREGNANCY?

A woman's uterus and ovaries work together as a unit. When a girl is born, her ovaries have thousands of ova (eggs) in them, each about the size of a grain of sand. From the time she begins to menstruate, one of these ova is expelled from an ovary every 28 days or thereabouts. It travels down the oviduct (Fallopian tube) to the uterus.

In the days just before an ovum is expelled, the lining of the uterus becomes thicker and spongier and is enriched with blood—ready to receive and nourish an ovum that has been fertilized by a male sperm.

If the fertilized ovum does not arrive, the thick, spongy lining is shed in the monthly period: this is menstruation. When a fertilized ovum does arrive, the lining is not shed and so the monthly periods stop during pregnancy.

After the baby is born, the process begins again, awaiting the arrival of another fertilized ovum.

12. ARE THERE SIGNS OF PREGNANCY THAT ONLY THE DOCTOR SEES?

Yes, the doctor will see that the cervix (the mouth of the uterus or womb) has become soft and elastic.

There are also a number of tests for pregnancy shortly after fertilization. In the Ascheim-Zondek (A-Z) test, a small sample of morning urine is injected into immature female mice. If the woman is pregnant, the hormones in her urine will cause the mouse ovaries to enlarge. The result is known in four to five days and is ninety-eight percent accurate.

The Friedman test—also about ninety-eight percent accurate—uses a rabbit and gives the answer in three days.

A still more sensitive test, the H.C.G. test—giving a diagnosis in two hours—has recently been developed. It uses specially treated red cells of sheep, plus the serum from the blood of a rabbit which has been treated with pregnancy hormones. If the woman is pregnant, the addition of a few drops of her urine to this special preparation will cause certain changes in it. This is very accurate—and immediate.

In the fifth month, the doctor can hear the baby's heartbeat. It is a faint rhythmic sound—usually between 130 and 140 beats a minute. Doctors used to think that they could tell whether the baby was a boy or a girl by the speed of the heartbeat: slower for boys, faster for girls. But this didn't prove true. So don't count on knowing the sex of your baby until you see him—or her.

As the baby grows, the doctor can begin to feel his outline through the abdominal wall; and in the last months you, too, may be able to feel the baby's head or arm or foot in the same way.

X ray reveals the presence of a baby in the uterus. But, because of the dangers of radiation, especially to unborn babies in early stages of development, X rays are not usually used to confirm pregnancy. Sometimes, in the very last weeks, the doctor safely uses X ray to measure the pelvis. He can see whether the size of the exit and the size of the baby are matched (see Question 41) and whether there is more than one baby.

13. WHY PRENATAL CARE?

A woman may feel "like a million" when she is expecting a baby. Her body is well equipped for this job. But it is doing extra work: she is breathing for the baby, supplying his food, removing his body wastes, keeping his temperature normal—and much more. This puts a tax on her heart, lungs, kidneys, muscles, general vitality and emotions.

For this reason it is important to see a doctor (or to visit a clinic) as soon as a woman thinks she is pregnant. The doctor keeps a watchful eye on all of her functions. He helps her over the little discomforts caused by bodily changes. By various tests, he learns how mother and baby are doing. If, by chance, something goes wrong, he can catch little troubles before they become big.

There is an extra dividend, too. In getting to know the doctor early in pregnancy, the mother and father develop confidence in him and his judgment, so that when the time for the baby's birthday rolls around, they are relaxed and ready.

Health History

When a mother goes to see the doctor for the first

time, he will ask many questions. He needs to know the answers if he is to help. He will ask about:

——the past health of expectant mother and father and of their parents;

——the menstrual history of the mother and whether she has ever been pregnant before—previous miscarriages, previous labors, etc.;

——the diseases the expectant mother has had during her life: scarlet fever, rheumatic fever, measles, mumps, diabetes, tuberculosis;

——accidents, broken bones.

Give him frank and complete answers.

From Top to Toe

Then the doctor completely examines the expectant mother, including: weight, blood pressure, eyes, ears, nose, throat, teeth, heart, lungs, breasts, abdomen, ankles, feet.

He will do an internal examination checking the vagina, cervix and uterus. This will be more comfortable if the mother relaxes as completely as possible by taking long, deep breaths.

Sometimes a doctor does not do all this the first time. He may spread out the examination over several visits. But he will make a number of tests in that first examination. These tests will tell him much about the state of the mother's health and enable him to do what is necessary to protect her and her baby:

Blood Tests

blood type
count of red and white blood cells
hemoglobin

Rh factor
a test for syphilis

Examination of Urine

to make sure the woman is pregnant (if there is any question)
to check functioning of kidneys

Papanicolau Test ("Pap Smear")

to find out if there are cancer cells in the birth canal

Some of these tests he will make only once. Others he will repeat every time she goes to see him. Usually the doctor likes an expectant mother to visit him every three or four weeks for the first six or seven months, and then every two weeks until the last month when visits are usually every week. At a clinic, the mother may see different doctors and nurses each time she goes, but they will have her record and provide the care that protects her and the baby.

Because childbearing is a family affair, there are many practical reasons why husbands should go with their wives to see the doctor on the first visit and, if possible, several times again.

14. HOW TO CHOOSE A DOCTOR AND HOSPITAL?

When a woman first suspects that a baby is coming, one of her first thoughts is naturally to see a doctor. But the question is: *what* doctor?

Private Physician: Semi-private or Private Care in a Hospital

If she wants her own doctor, there are three choices:
——a specialist who is certified by the American College of Obstetricians and Gynecologists;
——a general practitioner who spends a major part of his time on maternity care;
——her own family doctor.

The first time at the doctor's, the expectant mother usually wants to talk over with him the matters that are first in her thoughts. Some mothers, for instance, want to "take part" in the birth of their babies. They want to be as comfortable as possible but are ready to accept some discomfort or pain if it comes; they do not want to be "knocked out" by drugs. Others want to be completely unconscious when the baby is being born.

Some couples want to be together during labor. Some want to have the baby in the hospital room with the mother (rooming-in) for much of the time.

Make sure that your doctor understands what you want, can take you to a hospital where your wishes and needs will be met, and will cooperate with you as much as possible.

In the first interview, ask about fees. They vary in different parts of the country and within the same community. Husbands are especially concerned with whatever financial arrangements are being made.

Clinic Care

Hospitals in many communities provide clinic and ward services for a flat fee. This includes care during pregnancy, labor and delivery, and after the baby is born—usually terminating with a final examination at the end of six weeks.

In most big cities, municipal hospitals and some voluntary hospitals provide maternity care either at low cost or free (at public expense) if the patient can't pay. Sometimes a social worker or city investigator will make a study of a family's ability or inability to pay.

Clinics are often crowded, and the wait may be long, but the medical care is usually good. If a mother understands the situation, she will often find behind the wall of busyness a friendly doctor or nurse really trying to be of help. Go expecting to be there for several hours. If there are no lunch facilities, take a sandwich and fruit. Remember, seeing the doctor regularly is important to your health and your baby's. Plan to do this even if it means taking a day off from work regularly. Most clinics don't mind if children come with their mothers; some have play area facilities.

15. HOW IS A WOMAN LIKELY TO FEEL WHEN SHE IS EXPECTING A BABY?

In the First Three Months

How a mother will feel when she first suspects that she is pregnant depends to a great extent on her feelings about herself. Is she happy? Does she really want to have this baby—now? Does the coming of the baby upset career plans or work schedule? Will her stopping work so reduce the income that the family has to scrimp to get along?

It is important to face doubts, insecurities and fears as well as joys, hopes and dreams. Some mothers are ecstatic from the first. Others don't have much enthusiasm for the coming baby for some months. A woman who is reasonably content may have a new joy of living when she becomes pregnant. Some women have never felt better.

Disturbed? Talk it out together and with your doctor.

An expectant mother may tire more easily, cry more easily, laugh more easily, get upset more easily. Her skin and hair may become a problem; so may constipation and the need to urinate frequently. She may occasionally be troubled by nausea ("morning sickness") and heartburn. But all these quickly pass because . . .

In the Second Three Months

Doubts and fears and regrets usually begin to disappear. Fatigue and sleepiness vanish, and wives want to do things with their husbands and friends. Most of the early discomforts are gone—the nausea, heartburn and frequent urination.

The waistline begins to enlarge, and clothes become tighter. Don't go rushing off to buy a new wardrobe. Gradually get what is needed. Some women worry about their changing figures. They are even concerned that their husbands may lose interest in them. Remember, to most men, a pregnant woman has a special beauty of her own.

To most people, except a woman's best friends, the happy condition may not yet be noticeable. But the mother can begin to feel the growing uterus through the abdominal wall. She probably won't need rouge to heighten her color. Nature will do that job for her. The house often becomes too warm, the blankets on the bed too many. She may perspire freely. Hair grows faster, and her nails may be more brittle.

In the Third Three Months

Now the baby grows rapidly, and the mother shows it. At first, the baby is deep in her pelvis. But, as he grows, the uterus grows too, making her abdomen bigger and bigger. This is when good posture—standing, sitting, walking, lifting and lying—pays off in less fatigue and a more graceful *you* (see Question 19).

The baby is now kicking and moving around, especially at night. This is the time when some women begin to get those maternal feelings which they missed earlier in pregnancy. They dream about the baby. Will he (or she) be fair or dark? Whom will he look like?

By the eighth month or sooner, the baby will be so big and high that sometimes his mother becomes short of breath. She wonders if she can contain this baby for another month. Then, almost overnight, he sinks deeper into the pelvis, getting ready for the day of his birth. She can take a deep breath again. But back comes the problem of frequent urination. It is caused by the baby's weight pushing down on the bladder.

With all that extra weight the mother is carrying, her ankles may swell if she is on her feet too much. Resting with feet up several times a day can help.

16. OF WHAT VALUE ARE CLASSES FOR EXPECTANT MOTHERS AND FATHERS?

When a woman first learns that she is pregnant, she often looks ahead to the months of waiting and wonders just how she is going to cope with them. Then she and her husband go to class for expectant parents and they meet a group of people who are in the same situation. They may have similar—or different—questions and feelings about motherhood and fatherhood, but as they sit together and talk out their questions with a doctor or nurse, the road ahead will seem shorter and more certain (Fig. 30).

But more than that, a couple enrolled in a class for expectant parents learns such things as:

——how to make pregnancy as happy and healthful an experience as possible;

——facts about childbearing as a natural function that usually goes well;

——what the coming of a baby can mean to family life, to husband, wife and other children;

——how to take care of the baby;

——how to select medical, nursing and hospital care;

Fig. 30 At parents' class—a chance to talk out their questions with doctor or nurse.

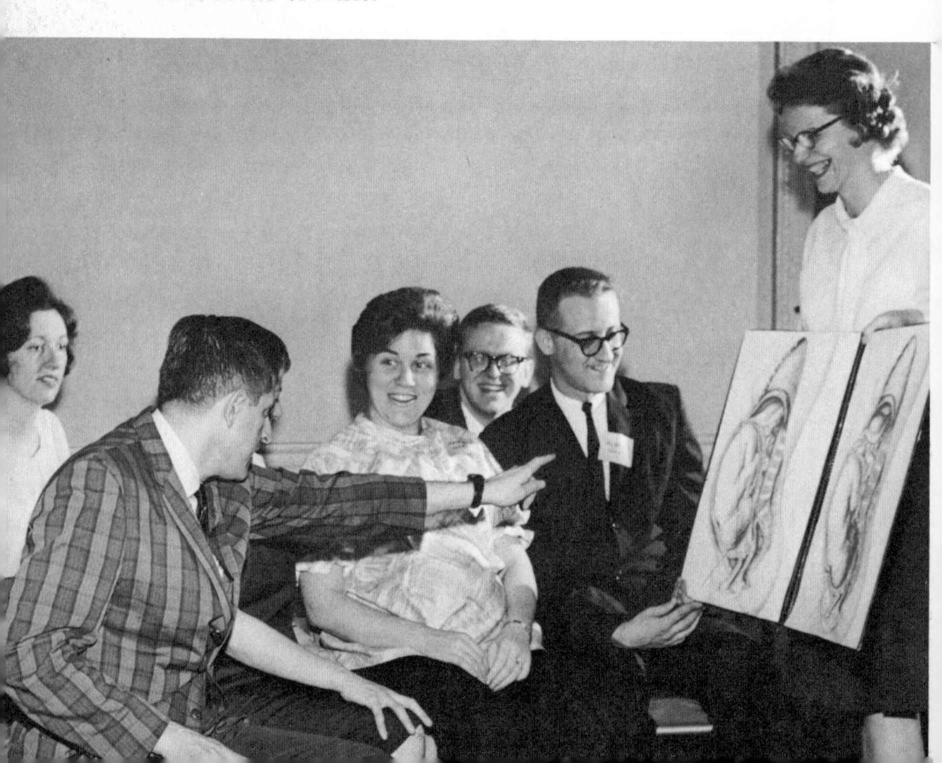

——how to budget time and money as the family grows;
——how to choose foods to keep a family healthy and trim.

For those who are interested in the psychophysical methods of childbearing—like *natural childbirth,* or the "Lamaze method," called *psychoprophylaxis,* or *hypnosis*—there is usually an opportunity to learn how to avoid stress during pregnancy and labor, how to breathe for relaxation during labor and delivery, and how to exercise for a quick comeback after the baby comes (Fig. 31).

To find out about classes in your community, ask your doctor or call your local visiting nurse association, Red Cross chapter, health department or hospital.

Fig. 31 Father learns in class how he can help.

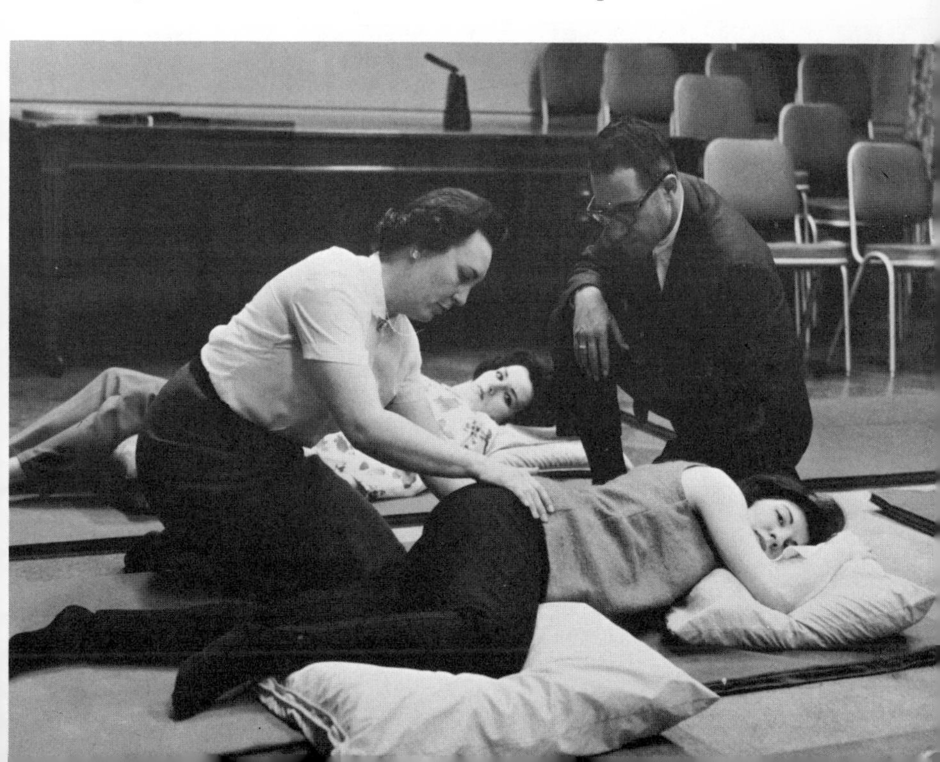

17. SHOULD AN EXPECTANT MOTHER CONTINUE TO WORK DURING PREGNANCY? FOR HOW LONG?

If the job is not too tiring or filled with nervous tension, a woman who enjoys working can stay with it during pregnancy, especially if several rest periods are possible during the day's work. Of course, if the expectant mother is a lady truck driver, air-hammer operator or circus acrobat, another job should be found. Jobs requiring only moderate physical work but long and tiring hours should be avoided; also jobs requiring delicate balance and constant standing.

Feel "bushed" every night? Then the time has come to quit. Whether "bushed" or not, most expectant mothers feel better if they stop work about six weeks before the baby is due.

And remember, a six-week rest period after the baby comes is also advisable. Don't go back to your job until the doctor says OK.

18. WHAT KIND OF MATERNITY CLOTHES ARE NECESSARY?

Any woman will find that dressing attractively during pregnancy is important to both her high spirits and her husband's. How we look has much to do with how we feel. Today's maternity clothes help the expectant mother to look trim and pretty.

Select your maternity wardrobe, however, with an eye to the future as well as to style—especially if this is your first baby and you hope to have more. Well-made clothing holds the shape even after long, hard wear. Of course, comfort is the first consideration, but attractiveness and style are also important and can go hand in hand with comfort.

When you go shopping, you'll be pleased at the wide selection of pretty maternity clothes—and at reasonable prices, too! There are good-looking dresses for everyday wear, well-cut slacks with loose tunic tops, dresses to wear shopping or to the beach and chic party clothes (Figs. 32, 33, 34, 35, 36).

If you practice good posture when standing, sitting and lying, you will probably never need a maternity girdle. If both you and your doctor feel a girdle would help to prevent that oh-my-aching-back feeling, it need not be an elaborate contraption. It should, however, be of the non-binding type, and it should do only one thing: support the baby as if you placed your two hands to hold up the uterus from below. This helps to keep the uterus in a straight up-and-down line. It takes the strain off the back and abdominal muscles and does not restrict the baby or your breathing. A maternity girdle is not a fashion garment to keep you looking in style during pregnancy.

Fig. 32 (Left) A sleeveless cotton bi-color shift with a coordinating gardening hat—cool and comfortable for everyday summer wear. Price about $25. *Courtesy of Lane Bryant*

Fig. 33 (Right) Scintillating silver 'night shirt' for the mother-to-be. Spacious shirt in shimmering horizontal stripes which shift to bias on jewel-buttoned tab and verticals on jewel-buttoned sleeves. Price $30. *Courtesy of Lane Bryant*

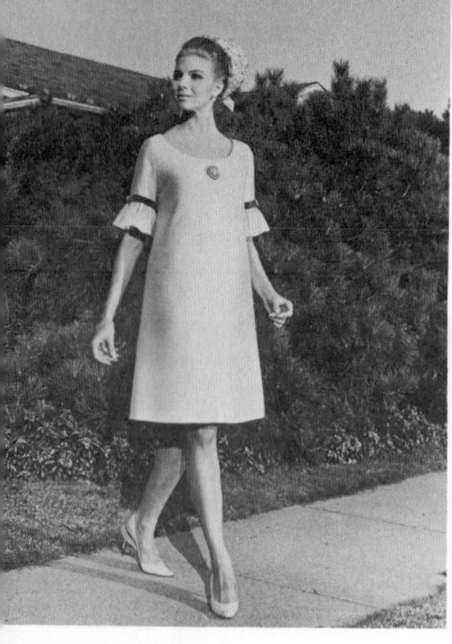

Fig. 34 The Empire bodice features a modified horseshoe neckline and falls freely to an A-line with lots of room for the growing baby. The elbow-length sleeves ruffle under the velvet trim and bow. Price about $15. *Courtesy of Lane Bryant*

Fig. 35 This sleeveless and low-turtle-neck blouse is made of ribbed cotton knit. The two-way nylon stretch slacks allow for growth and always fit comfortably. (Blouse priced at about $7; slacks, $9) *Courtesy of Lane Bryant*

A maternity bra is a matter of choice. Some mothers get several because of the comfort and extra support they offer.

As your baby grows bigger and your abdomen protrudes, your sense of balance is less certain. High heels tend to push your center of balance further forward, so you are less steady on your feet. In addition, high heels make you lean backward to maintain your balance. It's not a pretty position.

If you have worn high heels most of your adult life, flats may feel very queer indeed. In fact, wearing them may cause pain in your leg muscles. Fortunately, there are many gracefully shaped medium heels, and they

Fig. 36 A crisp white piqué shift trimmed with eyelet ruffles to make those hours of waiting a delight. Price about $16. *Courtesy of Lane Bryant*

are comfortable.

Of course, if you are going out to some special party where you won't be on your feet for any length of time, you may wear high heels. But don't stand a lot, and make sure of your balance when you rise and walk.

Your lingerie can be stretched out of shape as your figure changes. It is good to buy a maternity slip and specially cut maternity panties that grow with your waistline.

Your nails, skin and hair may need extra care. So don't omit the usual trips to the beauty shop. It is good relaxation and good for your morale.

Keeping Fit While Pregnant

19. WHAT IS THE SECRET OF KEEPING FIT DURING THE NINE MONTHS OF PREGNANCY?

Many expectant mothers complain of aching back and leg muscles, shortness of breath when climbing stairs, trouble finding a comfortable position when lying down, and feeling awkward when sitting, rising from a chair and walking.

Fig. 37 Sit when you can. *Photo by Larry Gordon Studios–Courtesy of Pepperell Mfg. Co.*

The secret for avoiding these minor discomforts of pregnancy and of keeping fit is rest and good posture. Every woman needs an increasing amount of rest as the baby grows heavier and puts an extra tax on her energy. This means stopping before becoming over-tired—putting up the feet and perhaps taking a brief catnap. In later pregnancy, it is good to lie down in the afternoon for an hour or so.

This doesn't mean treating oneself like an invalid. On the contrary, every day can be a joy. Make it so by sitting, standing, walking and lying in good posture.

Standing

Avoid standing when you can sit (Fig. 37); but, if you must stand, stand correctly (Fig. 38).

When waiting, it is better to walk back and forth than to stand.

When standing to use household equipment, the best position, if you are right-handed, is with the left leg forward (Fig. 39) so you can swing your body and shift weight from foot to foot.

Fig. 38 When you must stand, stand correctly.

Walking

In walking, start off in the correct standing position. Keep the back upright with the head up as if an invisible cord were pulling the top of the head toward the sky or ceiling.

Climbing Stairs

When climbing stairs, use the back foot (on lower step) to push off. Plant the front foot firmly on the step ahead and push off with the toe of the back foot, maintaining good posture (Fig. 40).

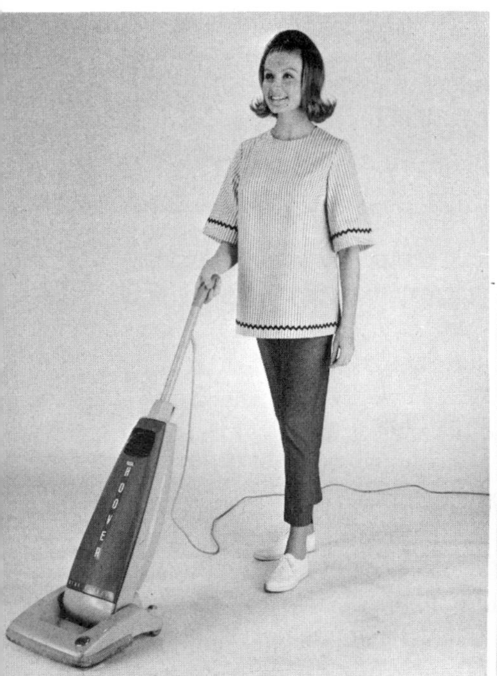

Fig. 39 Best position for using household equipment. *Photo by Larry Gordon Studios—Courtesy of Pepperell Mfg. Co.*

Fig. 40 Climbing stairs. *Photo by Larry Gordon Studios—Courtesy of Pepperell Mfg. Co.*

Fig. 41 Bending down to reach low objects. *Photo by Larry Gordon Studios*

Stooping and Lifting

The best advice about stooping is, *don't.* If you must reach to floor level, squat with your back straight and your hips flexed. Whenever possible, your legs should be used to spare your back.

To reach something immediately in front, squat with the feet level (Fig. 41).

For something to the side, squat sideways with one leg in front of the other (Fig. 42).

In all squatting, the back should be straight and the knees far enough apart to leave room for the abdomen without squeezing.

When lifting is unavoidable, if the object is at floor level, get close to it and use your legs—not your back—to take the strain. Hold the object close while rising (Figs. 43 and 44).

To lift from the side, advance the leg on the opposite side, bend the knees to grasp the object, hold it close and rise to full height. When a child needs or wants to be lifted, you can often help him to scramble up, using his own legs, while you stand behind him and guide him (Fig. 45).

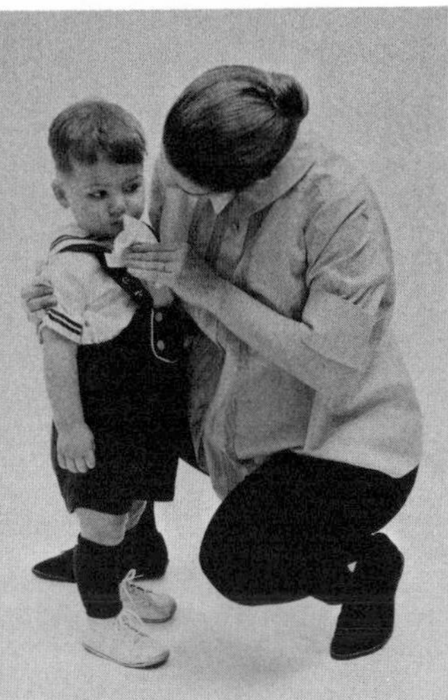

Fig. 42 Another good position to use when you bend down.

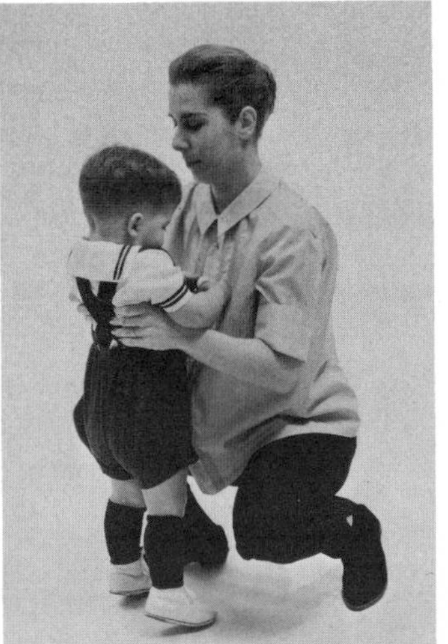

Fig. 43 When you lift something from the ground, start in this position.

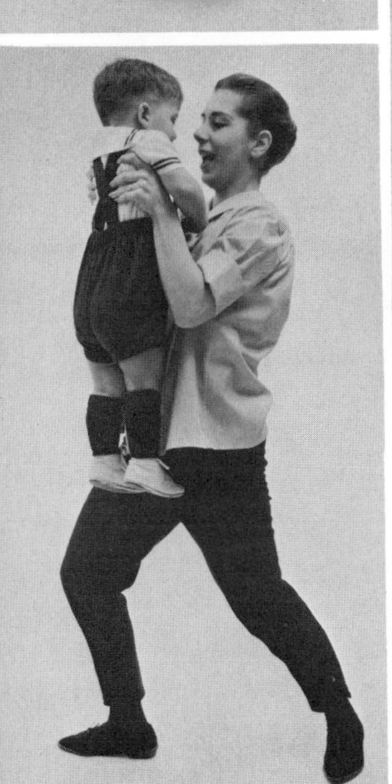

Fig. 44 Stand properly with feet apart to give support as you lift.

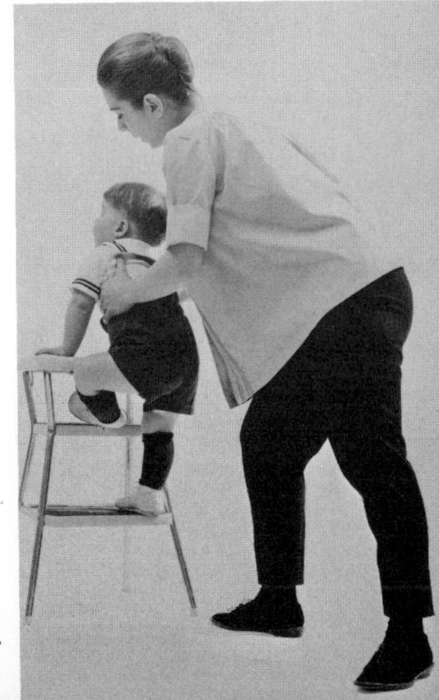

Fig. 45 Avoid straining when you bend to lift.

Carrying

Keep both shoulders level (Fig. 46). If the load is so heavy that it tilts the shoulders, divide it in two, if possible, and carry half in each hand. Use a shopping cart for heavy loads whenever possible (Fig. 47).

Sitting

Choose a good chair to sit comfortably. The seat should be low enough to allow both feet to rest comfortably on the floor (Fig. 48); if the seat is too high, rest your feet on a low foot stool. The seat should be deep enough to support the full length of your thighs

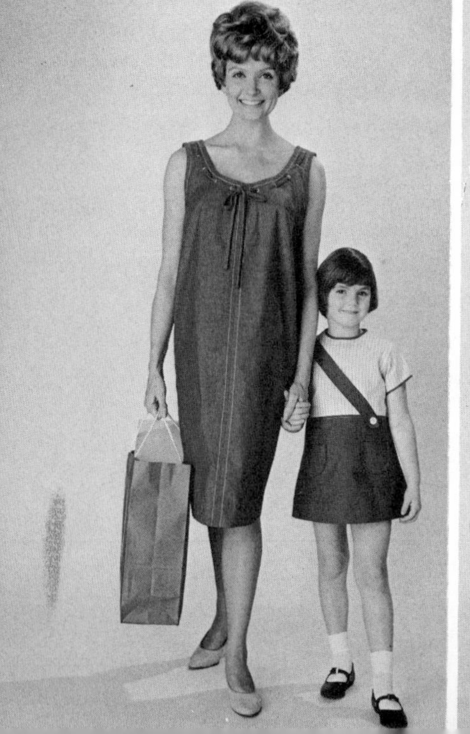

Fig. 46 Best method for carrying bundles. *Photo by Larry Gordon Studios*

Fig. 47 If your packages are heavy, use a cart to transport them. *Photo by Larry Gordon Studios*

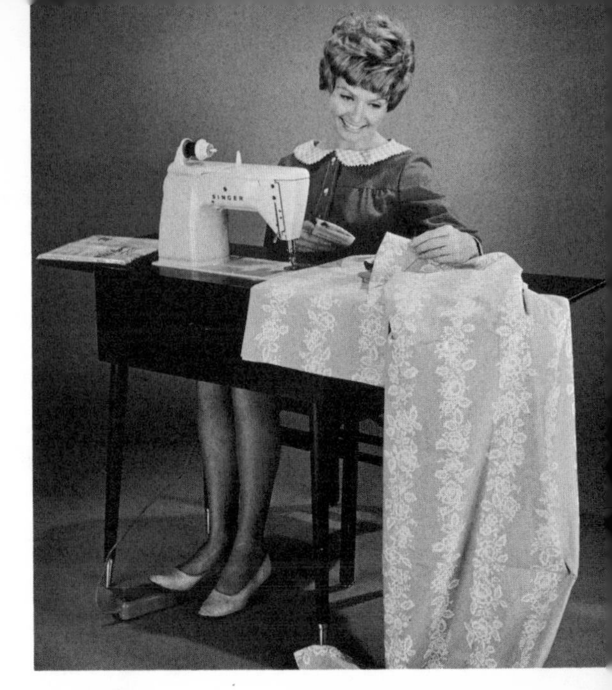

Fig. 48 Maintain good posture when sitting. *Photo by Larry Gordon Studios*

and allow you to get all the way in, so the back of the chair supports your back. If the chair has arms, they should be high enough to support your arms without tension in your shoulders.

To get into a chair gracefully, stand in front of it with one foot slightly before the other, the back knee touching the edge of the chair. Bend knees and use leg muscles to lower body to chair seat. Bend your body slightly forward, with back straight and muscles of abdomen and buttocks contracted. Sit tall with weight evenly distributed on both buttocks.

To rise, put one foot slightly in front of the other, slide buttocks to edge of chair and push off with back foot, using leg muscles to raise body. Assume good posture before starting to walk.

You can rest in a comfortable chair with your legs elevated. Put a pillow under your knees and keep heels higher than buttocks (Fig. 49).

Fig. 49 Whenever possible, sit with your feet raised and supported.

Fig. 50 Best position for kneeling.

Change of Posture

During pregnancy, frequent change of position is good to avoid congestion and long, continued pressure on nerves and veins. Remember to move about often. When doing something at ground level, you will find that a kneeling posture often proves comfortable (Fig. 50).

Height of Work Surfaces

Since work surfaces in homes are usually of standard height and not planned for short or tall people, some thought should be given to making adjustments to reduce the need to stoop or stretch. Handles may be shortened or lengthened as necessary. Racks may be placed in sinks or on tables if the work surface is too low. Or you can stand on a well-placed sturdy bench if the work surface is too high.

In selecting new equipment, keep comfortable work heights in mind. Surfaces for bathing or changing the baby should be at the mother's hip level (Fig. 51). When buying a baby carriage make sure that the handle is at a comfortable height, and that it is easy to see over the hood (Fig. 52).

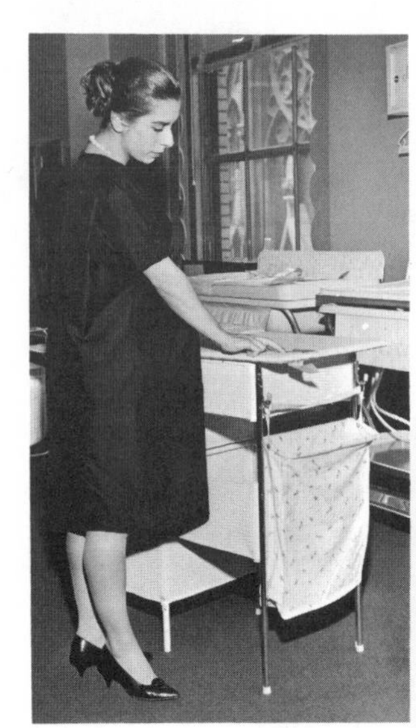

Fig. 51 Make certain that work areas are adjusted to the proper level for you.

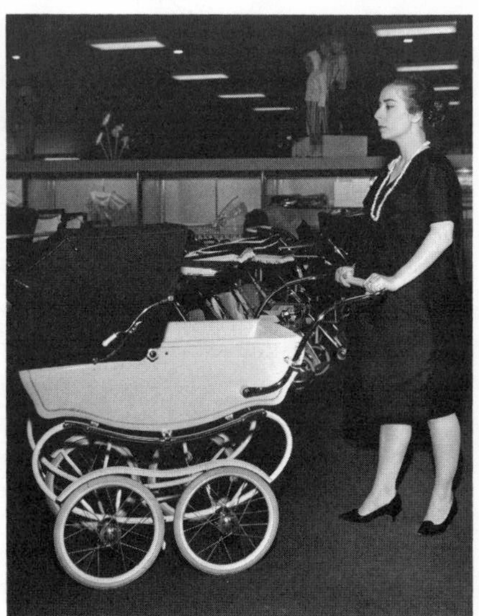

Fig. 52 Choose a baby carriage with a handle level right for you.

Lying Comfortably in Bed

Lying in bed can be comfortable even in the last months when your abdomen seems large and protruding. Lie on your side with all muscles limp and loose and the baby's weight resting on the bed. The positions in the pictures are comfortable for most pregnant women (Figs. 53 and 54).

Fig. 53 Find the most comfortable sleeping position.

Fig. 54 Another comfortable sleeping posture.

20. "MORNING SICKNESS"—WHAT TO DO ABOUT IT?

One of the first signs of pregnancy may be that an expectant mother has "morning sickness" when she gets out of bed. She may lose her breakfast, but soon she feels OK. As the weeks pass, so usually does the morning sickness.

Doctors don't know the exact cause. It may be due to some body changes that come with pregnancy. It may occur because the mother is emotionally upset; or just because she may expect to be sick. That doesn't mean that morning sickness is "all mental." The doctor always wants to know about it. He may be able to prescribe something that quiets a queasy stomach.

Don't get upset about it. This will pass. In the meantime: a few dry crackers while still in bed in the morning; smaller meals more often during the day; no greasy foods.

21. THAT OVERTIRED FEELING—WHAT TO DO ABOUT IT?

Nobody should get overtired, especially an expectant mother. Getting enough rest is the key to not feeling "done in," but there is a special kind of tiredness in the early months of pregnancy.

The mother may suddenly feel fatigued as if someone had pulled the stopper out of her reserve of energy and drained it away. When dinner is over and the dishes are washed and hubby settles down for a quiet talk, she may yawn in his face and go sound asleep. But if she gets extra rest during the day—at home or on the job—she'll be ready to be a good companion after dinner. This is important to her health and the comfort of the family.

22. CONSTIPATION—WHAT TO DO ABOUT IT?

Constipation is often a problem to women during pregnancy. Don't try to solve it by taking a laxative, unless the doctor says *yes*. Often a change in diet can solve the problem. White bread, crackers, candy and "pop" leave little "bulk" to stimulate the digestive tract. If you have been eating much of these foods, replace them with whole grain cereals, dried fruits, fresh fruits and vegetables (especially raw ones). Take a little exercise, perhaps a daily walk, and set aside a regular time for elimination every day—and you'll be surprised at the difference.

23. CRAMPS IN THE LEGS AND FEET—WHAT TO DO ABOUT THEM?

Cramps are often caused by too much phosphorus in the diet. A woman with bothersome cramps should speak to her doctor about them. He may recommend reducing the amount of milk taken as it contains much phosphorus. Or, if he still advises drinking milk because it contains the calcium so necessary for the baby's strong bones and teeth, he may prescribe a medicine to remove some of the phosphorus from the mother's digestive tract.

Cramps can often be prevented by positions and movements designed to improve circulation in the legs and feet. Women usually get temporary relief by stretching the cramped muscles.

For common cramps in the calf, rest your foot on a step or chair with the heel free. Bend your trunk forward slightly, keeping the knee braced so the cramped muscle is stretched. *Do not rub!*

Another method is to extend the leg on the bed while

your husband applies pressure on the top of the knee with one hand and bends the foot upward with the other.

24. HEARTBURN—WHAT TO DO ABOUT IT?

Heartburn, that burning feeling in the back of the throat, is not always due to acid, as many people think. Taking sodium bicarb won't help at all. In fact, it may create other problems. If you have heartburn frequently, talk to your doctor about it.

Heartburn in pregnancy is often caused by slower emptying of the stomach, with the food backing up. Best precaution against occasional discomfort: don't overeat. Eat smaller and more frequent meals. Eat slowly and chew your food well. Serve meals attractively, and keep the atmosphere at the table happy. Fatigue, worry and emotional strain are often factors in indigestion.

Discomfort following meals may be reduced by eliminating or decreasing the amount of such foods as:

Gas-forming vegetables and fruits
cabbage, onions, garlic, radishes, cucumbers, peppers, dried peas and beans, cauliflower, turnips, rutabagas, cantaloupe, watermelon

Very fatty foods
fried foods, gravies, salad dressings, pastries, nuts, cheese (except cottage cheese), fatty meats, oily fish

Fig. 55 Exercise to keep muscles toned.

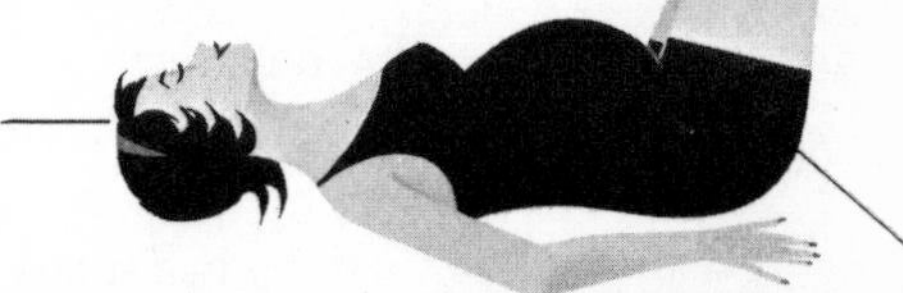

Starchy foods
macaroni, spaghetti, rice, cereals and bread (except in small portions)
Highly seasoned and spicy foods
pepper, mustard, chili powder, horseradish, meat sauce, catsup, pickles, olives
Sweets
candy, jams, jellies, sugar (except in limited amounts), rich puddings, molasses
Coffee and tea, with sugar and cream

Not all of these foods may cause distress in any one person. Experience will tell you which foods to avoid.

25. VARICOSE VEINS—WHAT TO DO ABOUT THEM?

Varicose veins are sometimes a great bother to women during the last three months. The extra weight of the baby causes pressure on the blood vessels of the legs, and cuts down on the circulation. The best way to lessen this pressure is to get off your feet as often as possible, elevating the legs or hips during the rest period (see Fig. 49). Before going to bed, lie for five minutes or longer in the position shown in Figure 55.

Don't wear tight clothing, especially a constricting girdle or round, elastic garters. These add to the circulation problem. Instead, try a garter belt.

26. BACKACHE—WHAT TO DO ABOUT IT?

Most lower backache in pregnancy disappears when the woman stands and sits correctly (see Question 19). A modified kneeling posture may help to relieve the pressure which causes backache and, sometimes, cramps in the legs (Fig. 56). This position should be maintained for only a minute or two—less if it causes discomfort, particularly in the abdominal wall—but it may be repeated many times during the day.

If the backache is higher up, and is combined with tingling or numbness in the fingers, improving the way the head and shoulders are held can help (Fig 57). Wearing a properly fitted, supportive bra with wide, non-constrictive straps may also help.

Ladies, don't sit in the same position (knitting in an armchair, for instance) for a long time.

Strengthen upper back muscles and the muscles that raise the shoulders by the exercise shown in Figure 57.

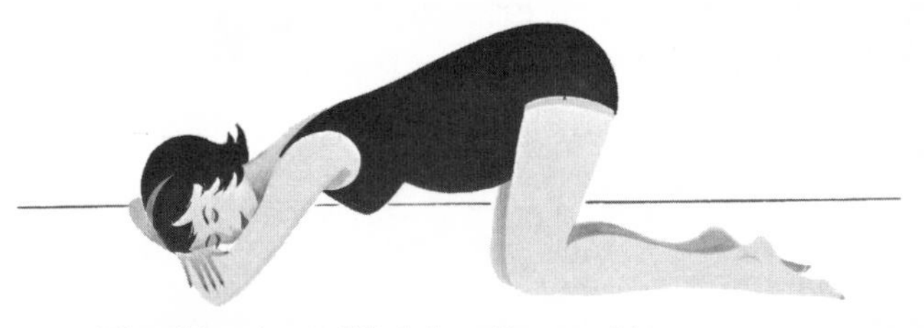

Fig. 56 A modified kneeling position.

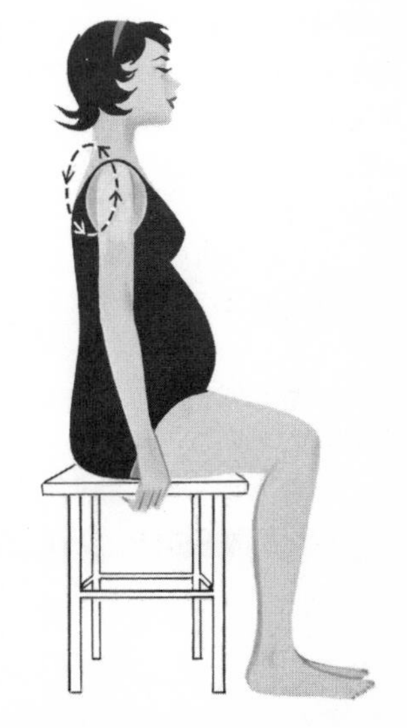

Fig. 57 Learn to sit properly.

27. IS IT ALL RIGHT TO HAVE SEXUAL RELATIONS DURING PREGNANCY?

Throughout most of pregnancy, there is no reason to change habits of sexual relations unless the doctor advises it. Some women may find that intercourse is less satisfying, and their desire for it may decrease. Others may have increased desire.

The usual positions for sexual relations may become uncomfortable as pregnancy progresses and the abdomen enlarges. Husband and wife may find that intercourse is more satisfactory when the woman lies on her side.

While some doctors make no rules about intercourse during the latter months, it is generally believed that sexual relations should be discontinued during the last six to eight weeks of pregnancy.

28. WHAT ABOUT BATHING IN THE LAST MONTHS OF PREGNANCY?

Mothers can enjoy a daily shower or bath throughout pregnancy and after the baby comes. For those who like to relax in a tub bath, a few suggestions: not too hot, and remember that during the last months the shift in the center of gravity makes balance more difficult. So, be careful when you're getting in and out of the slippery tub or shower. A mat in the tub is a good safety measure.

The old idea that wash water enters the vagina and carries infection to the uterus has been disproved.

29. WHY ARE DOCTORS SO STRICT ABOUT THE WEIGHT A MOTHER GAINS DURING PREGNANCY?

Many women gain too much weight during pregnancy. Excess weight can lead to difficulty, and the doctor is keenly aware of this. He will watch an expectant mother's weight when she comes to see him regularly during pregnancy. He may insist that she eat less, but will make sure not to upset the right balance of foods which are the building blocks for the new baby's body.

Sometimes he will tell the mother that she must cut down on salt. Salt intake may cause the body to retain too much water, resulting in the swelling of her face, ankles, feet, hands, and fingers. If not controlled, this can lead to a dangerous condition—toxemia.

The doctor's restrictions may be mild. He may say not to use extra salt on food, and to avoid salty foods, such as salted nuts and crackers, potato chips, ham, and bacon. But, if the signs show that a more drastic cut in salt is needed, he may be much more strict.

Salt is harmful at a time like this because it contains a mineral, sodium, which is also supplied by many foods which do not taste salty. The doctor may recommend using special products, such as low-sodium milk, low-sodium bread, and low-sodium butter. All kinds of "soda pop" contain sodium. And one thing definitely off the list is sodium bicarbonate, a common "home remedy" for indigestion. For helpful hints on restricting sodium in the diet, see the section at the end of this book on choosing the right foods.

The average woman may gain from twenty to twenty-two pounds during the nine months. This is accounted for as follows:

Baby	7½ lbs.
Placenta	1
Amniotic fluid	1½
Breasts	3

Uterus	2½
Blood volume	4
Water	2½

In the first three months, a mother usually gains from zero to three pounds; in the second three months, one-half pound a week; in the third three months, one pound a week.

The old idea that a mother needs to eat for two has been disproved. A pregnant woman's body makes better use of food.

30. HOW CAN A MOTHER KEEP HER WEIGHT DOWN AND STILL PROVIDE THE NECESSARY FOOD FOR HERSELF AND HER UNBORN, GROWING BABY?

When a woman becomes pregnant, what she eats affects not only her health and disposition but also her growing baby. He depends for his growth upon what his mother eats.

If she was eating properly before she became pregnant, she won't have to change her food habits in the first half of pregnancy. But if the diet was poor, NOW is the time to change.

Some women deprive themselves and their unborn babies of health-protecting foods by eating "slimming foods" that may be excellent in themselves but don't have the right balance for health. Many teenage mothers carry over their schooltime habits and fill up on hot dogs, malteds, soda pop and potato chips. Then there is no room for the protective salads and other important foods at mealtime.

A pregnant woman needs to eat enough of the *right* foods to provide the necessary building blocks for every new cell in her growing baby's body and to keep herself healthy and peppy. These same foods won't do Dad any harm either!

Nutritional Building Blocks

Every food provides some chemical for the growth, maintenance and repair of the body. Most of us eat because we like food, not because it has so many grams of protein, calcium or what-have-you. But it is always good to keep these values in mind as we make our daily selection. The most important of these food values are:

Calories: Just as an automobile needs fuel, so does the human body. The human fuel is found in proteins, starches, sugar and fats. All of us must have our quota of fuel or the human engine sputters and stalls. Many foods contain a number of essential food elements *and* calories. Others contain little but calories—someone has called them "lone wolf calories"—such as alcohol, candy, chocolate malteds, cokes. Drop these from your diet.

Protein: Best sources—meat, fish, poultry, eggs and dairy products. Protein is an essential in every cell of the body. It is a basic ingredient of the blood, of the antibodies with which to fight infections, of the hormones (several of which are essential for the continuance of pregnancy), of enzymes for good digestion, and many other body functions.

Calcium: Best sources—milk and other dairy products. This mineral is the chief building block for strong bones and teeth. It is needed by all the cells of the body. It helps to clot the blood, to contract muscles and to control the beating of the heart.

Iron: Sources—red meat, liver, eggs, potatoes, fruits, green vegetables, and enriched cereals. Iron is needed for the formation of hemoglobin in the blood, which carries life-giving oxygen to all parts of the body and takes away carbon dioxide, a body waste.

The baby in the uterus stores iron in his liver during the last three months because milk, his principal food for some time after his birth, contains almost no iron.

Vitamin A: Sources—liver, eggs, butter, and cheese. It is necessary for cell growth, development of bone structure, tooth formation, breast milk and healthy skin. It also helps to reduce susceptibility to infection.

Thiamine (Vitamin B1): Sources—whole grain cereals, beans, peas, beef, pork, liver, and nuts. Thiamine cannot be stored, so it is important to resupply the body every day. It promotes the baby's growth and stimulates the mother's appetite.

Riboflavin (Vitamin B2): Sources—milk, liver, kidney, fish, eggs, green leafy vegetables, and tomatoes. It, like thiamine, is not stored in the body. Riboflavin promotes energy and is essential for normal muscle activity.

Niacin: Chief sources—liver, lean meats, poultry, and fish. It protects the skin, the mucous membranes and the nerves.

Vitamin C: Sources—oranges, grapefruit, lemons and limes, raw vegetables, and tomatoes. It helps to keep the walls of the capillaries (the small blood vessels) strong, and is an essential element in the body cement which holds together cartilage, bones, muscles, and other tissues. Vitamin C contributes to the healing of wounds.

Vitamin D: Best source is sunlight. Scarce in natural foods. Chief food sources—milk, eggs, butter, cheese, fresh green vegetables, and vitamin-enriched margarine. It helps the body to use calcium and phosphorus efficiently.

How to eat the right combination every day? The New York State Health Department's Bureau of Nutrition puts it like this:

This very short story
Gives some of the clues
To eating for health,
And the best food to choose.

We start off with protein—
That's milk, eggs and meat,
Also cheese, poultry, seafood.
On this we don't cheat.

The fruits and the vegetables,
Some raw and some cooked,
Were grouped in three sections
Wherever we looked.

Be sure to include
Both cereal and bread
The dark or enriched kinds
Are way out ahead.

Some butter and cream,
Some sugar and spice,

Add flavor to food,
Help make your meals nice.

For more details on meal planning, see the suggestions at the end of this book, or buy the paperback book, *Food Becomes You,* by Ruth M. Leverton, published by Dolphin Book Section, Doubleday & Co., Inc., 95 cents.

31. HUNGRY ALL THE TIME? WHAT CAN A MOTHER DO ABOUT IT?

What a problem! The doctor warns you against overweight, and you are continually hungry. Try dividing your daily food into a number of smaller but more frequent meals. If you prefer "three squares" a day, reduce your main meals and have such foods as milk, fruit, or bread as in-between snacks. Or try raw carrots or celery sticks when you are hungry. They won't add much to your calories and may satisfy that urge to eat something.

32. ARE THERE ANY DON'TS IN PREGNANCY?

Nobody likes *don'ts,* and this is especially true for an expectant mother. The best rule is—enjoy life, but don't overdo. You may feel very well, but the margin between health and illness is thinner while you are carrying a baby.

So, it's *not too much* exercise, food, fun, sleep, drinking, smoking, etc. Any activity that causes jars and jolts, sudden speedups or slowdowns, or the likelihood of injury, should be avoided. This means no swan diving from a high tower—or a low diving board, for that matter. No ocean bathing where the waves are high and rough. No riding in a roller coaster or in any similar amusement park rides. No riding in a jeep over rough country.

What about horseback riding, golf, tennis, bowling, or similar sports? Yes, if you use common sense. Horseback riding is possible at a slow pace but don't play tennis or golf to the point of exhaustion.

There is no reason to become unduly concerned about losing the baby. He is well packaged in the uterus, and it is very difficult to shake him loose. Outermost is the mother's skin, then come the muscles of the abdominal wall; next is the uterus, thick and strong and lined with elastic membranes. Finally is the amniotic fluid (the bag of waters) in which the baby floats. All these absorb the everyday bumps, jolts, and vibrations.

Dr. Carl T. Javert, a New York obstetrician, believes that it is lack of physical and mental activity in our modern civilization, rather than overactivity, that is responsible for miscarriage (spontaneous abortion). He asked seven professors of obstetrics how many miscarriages due to overexertion they had seen in their years of experience. Four of them could not recall a single case.

This does not mean, if a mother is spotting or has had a series of spontaneous abortions, that she should help with the family moving. She is a special case, and needs the doctor's continuous advice and care.

33. ARE THERE DANGER SIGNS TO BE ON THE LOOKOUT FOR?

Childbearing is natural—and is usually normal. But sometimes things do go wrong, and it is good to be on the alert. Report *at once* to the doctor any of the following signs:

bleeding from the vagina, no matter how slight
swelling of face, fingers or ankles
severe, continuous headache
dimness or blurring of vision
pain in the abdomen
persistent vomiting
chills and fever
escape of fluid from vagina
baby stops moving

34. IS IT SAFE FOR A WOMAN TO SMOKE OR DRINK DURING PREGNANCY?

If you cannot stop smoking, cut down on the amount.

A reasonable number of cigarettes—say, ten a day or fewer—does not seem to harm the baby.

If you are accustomed to drinking, a highball or a glass of beer now and then doesn't do any harm. Alcohol in large amounts, however, is not good.

35. ARE ANY MEDICINES SAFE FOR A WOMAN TO TAKE "ON HER OWN" DURING PREGNANCY?

There are more than a dozen known drugs that can injure the baby in the uterus, and the list is growing. In recent years, thousands of unborn babies in Europe and Asia were crippled by a sleeping pill—thalidomide. This was a widely publicized tragedy. But many people do not recognize that they are using drugs, as Dr. Allan C. Barnes, Professor of Obstetrics at Johns Hopkins University, warns. For instance, the housewife who sprays her kitchen with a bug killer is not taking drugs in the usual sense, but inhaling this powerful bug killer can affect her unborn baby.

He also points out that the woman who forgets to take her birth-control pill once and gets pregnant on that particular night may damage her newly formed baby by using the pills again before she knows that she is pregnant.

Dr. Barnes says that a woman in the childbearing years should "practice therapeutic nihilism," which is another way of saying don't take anything—even the usual household remedies—unless, of course, the doctor prescribes it.

36. WHAT IS THE RH FACTOR? WHEN AND HOW DOES IT AFFECT BABY AND MOTHER?

The Rh factor is a chemical substance which is usually present in red blood cells. Those who have this factor in their blood are Rh positive. If they don't have it, they are Rh negative. This is unchanging throughout life. About eighty-five percent of the white race, ninety-two percent of the Negro race and nearly one hundred percent of the yellow race have the Rh factor.

Everybody's blood has the power to produce antibodies which are disease-fighters. If germs enter the body and start an infection, antibodies rush to the scene and kill the invaders. The unborn baby can be affected by the Rh factor in the following ways.

If the mother is Rh negative and the father is Rh positive, chances are the baby will be Rh positive. So the mother's Rh negative blood will make antibodies that attack the baby's Rh positive blood cells as if they were infectious invaders.

Fortunately, the mother's and baby's bloodstreams do not normally mix; each circulation is separate. But little leaks do occur in the placenta where the two bloodstreams are separated by a very thin wall.

If there is intermingling of mother's and baby's blood, some of the baby's red blood cells are destroyed by the mother's antibodies. The baby, therefore, develops anemia while in the womb. The mother is not affected—only the baby.

Most Rh negative mothers, unless they have had transfusions of positive blood earlier in life, do not have antibodies against Rh positive blood when they become pregnant for the first time. It is only after several pregnancies that they develop antibodies against Rh positive blood. Then every baby they have runs increasing risks.

If the expectant mother is Rh negative, the doctor tests her blood or the fluid in the bag of waters from time to time to find out if antibodies are forming. Medical science is developing ways to reduce antibody formation, making it increasingly important for her to be under the doctor's care. And now, medical science is also learning how to save an unborn baby's life by transfusions. As a last resort, the doctor may deliver the baby ahead of time.

An Rh negative mother need not be overconcerned. Only about one out of twelve Rh negative mothers ever becomes sensitized to her baby's blood. In addition, a new serum (anti-Rh gamma globulin), which has been described as "among the great medical accomplishments in obstetrical history," has been widely tested and found completely safe and effective. It has therefore been approved by the Federal Food and Drug Administration. The serum will be injected into the Rh negative mother within 72 hours after she gives birth to her first baby and will prevent the formation of antibodies against Rh positive blood. She will therefore be able to have future babies without fear.

37. WHAT ARE THE DARK "STRETCH" MARKS ON A PREGNANT WOMAN'S ABDOMEN?

In the latter months of pregnancy, dark, slightly depressed streaks often develop on the skin of the abdomen, and sometimes on the breasts and thighs. They are called *striae,* and are due to an excess of the hormones of pregnancy. They are *not* caused by the stretching of the skin, as used to be thought.

After the baby is born, these dark lines fade. But during subsequent pregnancies, they usually reappear as glistening, silvery lines.

38. WHAT ABOUT THE MOTHER WHO TRIED TO LOSE HER BABY IN EARLY PREGNANCY—COULD SHE HAVE HURT THE BABY?

A woman may be shocked when she first learns that she is pregnant. Instead of a welling-up of happy feeling, there may be impatience or desperation. *"Oh, I don't want the baby!"* she may wail to her husband or the doctor. She may want to have three or four children *later,* but not this one—not now! For the moment, other feelings may be more compelling. Sometimes it may be the man who reacts this way.

This is not a feeling to be ashamed of. Many parents early in pregnancy experience what the psychologists call *ambivalence,* having two contradictory feelings at the same time.

Today, many young marrieds work. Together, husband and wife bring home a good income. The woman wants a "fling at a career." They are enjoying life together, with no other responsibilities.

Then comes the recognition of pregnancy! To make matters worse, when husband and wife begin to look at their budget and the loss of nearly half their income, they feel trapped. This may cause physical upset in the woman—nausea and vomiting, headache, stomach ache, backache. Sometimes the husband has the same feelings.

Some couples do all sorts of things to cause a miscarriage. But a well-implanted baby is pretty hard to dislodge, and most old-fashioned "home remedies" do not work.

At the fifth month, the baby begins to make himself obvious. There are the first flutters of movement, and the doctor lets the mother hear the baby's heartbeat. Then she starts to worry, "Did I hurt the baby?"

The chances are that she didn't. Fortunately, a baby's most sensitive period of development is *before* a woman knows that she is pregnant. That is when all the important parts of his body are being formed. By the fifth or sixth week, the vital parts of the baby are completed. Of course, all the months of pregnancy are important, but, for the baby's development, not nearly so critical as the first few weeks.

By the fifth week, the baby is well protected in his secure, watery home. Once the placenta is mature and he is getting what he needs from his mother's bloodstream, the baby lives and thrives.

39. IF A PREGNANT WOMAN FALLS, WILL THE BABY BE HURT?

The baby is so well protected by the shock-absorbing bag of waters surrounding him and by the strong bony walls of the mother's pelvis that chances of injury if his mother falls are very few. But don't risk even that remote possibility by wearing high heels in the latter months of pregnancy—or by insisting on skiing or fancy ice-skating or high diving. Remember, you have no shock absorbers around *you,* and your balance is different! Bathtubs are especially dangerous; use a mat and, if possible, a hand support; then be sure to get out of the tub slowly and carefully, making sure not to slip.

40. IS THERE DANGER TO THE BABY IF THE MOTHER IS EXPOSED TO GERMAN (3-DAY) MEASLES DURING PREGNANCY?

You may have heard about the dangers to the unborn baby if a mother contracts German measles while she is pregnant.

If you think that you may have been exposed to German measles, remember these facts:

——If a mother is exposed after she knows that she is pregnant, the worst danger period is over. The chief damage is done to babies while their basic body elements are being laid down in the weeks before a woman misses her first menstrual period.

——Babies are seldom damaged if their mothers get German measles after the twelfth week.

——A fast, easy, inexpensive blood test has recently been developed by scientists at the National Institutes of Health to tell if a mother who has been exposed to the disease has actually been infected. This should set many minds at rest. If it is found that the mother has been infected, the doctor and mother have the facts on which to make a decision as to whether she should continue her pregnancy.

Within a short time, the threat of German measles may be conquered. Two doctors at the National Institutes of Health (NIH) in Bethesda, Maryland (Drs. Harry M. Meyer, Jr. and Paul D. Parkman), have developed a vaccine which they believe can protect a person against *ever* contracting German measles. It can be given to young children, and their immunity should last for life. It can also be given to young married women and expectant mothers who have never had German measles. The NIH scientists predict that the vaccine will be ready to combat the next outbreak of the disease, which is not expected until the early 1970s.

41. SHOULD A MOTHER HAVE X RAYS DURING PREGNANCY?

Women in childbearing years—say, from fourteen to fifty—should be wary of X ray. Medical studies have shown that X rays, especially of the lower abdomen, can damage the ova from which a baby may grow, and can do serious damage to a fertilized ovum or to a baby in its earliest stages of development—even before the woman knows that she is pregnant.

Radiation adds up in life. That is, every time a person is exposed to radiation in any form, it has an effect on the body. The effect of each dose is added to the other previous doses. Under proper conditions, however, X ray is an important device that the doctor uses to diagnose and to treat disease—and it might save your life. Doctors know what is a dangerous dose of X ray, and X-ray technicians can shield the sex organs from damage. No woman should be refused or refuse the wonderful benefits of X-ray diagnosis or treatment because of a slight possibility of damage to the baby.

Experts often postpone necessary X-ray tests until late in pregnancy to avoid damage to the baby. If a woman in the childbearing years is not pregnant, she is usually X-rayed only during the two weeks following her menstrual periods.

42. IF A MOTHER TAKES NARCOTICS—DRUGS, "DOPE"—DURING PREGNANCY, WILL HER BABY BE "HOOKED"?

Yes, the baby will be addicted. Chances are it will

be premature and have to fight for its life. Soon after birth, it will show withdrawal symptoms. Under good care in a hospital, the baby may be saved, but this is, indeed, a poor start in life.

An addicted mother, herself, may have difficulties during pregnancy and labor. Her physical condition is usually poor, and she does not care about improving it. When labor begins, she often delays going into the hospital, making an emergency out of an event in life that is natural and usually is normal.

In the Last Weeks of Pregnancy

43. WHAT SHOULD THE MOTHER HAVE READY TO TAKE TO THE HOSPITAL?

Pack your bag a month in advance for a quick take-off. Put in it:

- robe, slippers, nightgown, bed jacket
- toilet articles and cosmetics
- shower cap
- sanitary belt
- writing paper, envelopes, pen or pencil, stamps
- change for telephone calls
- something to amuse you—book, magazines, deck of cards, knitting, embroidery, etc.

44. WHAT SHOULD THE FATHER HAVE READY FOR THE TRIP TO THE HOSPITAL?

Father should have handy a list with the following information: name and telephone number of doctor; name and telephone number of hospital; name and telephone number of taxi company, if you don't have a car. Prepare further by asking yourself the following questions:

Do you know who will take care of the other children, if you leave the house with your wife in the middle of the night?

Do you have enough gas in your car?

Do you have money for the taxi?

Do you know your way to the hospital, and where the parking facilities are?

Do you know which entrance of the hospital is open at all times of day and night?

Do you have your Blue Cross or other insurance identification card?

Do you know how to call an ambulance in your community?

Do you have all this written down—so that your wife can use it if you are not at home?

45. HOW CAN THE MOTHER TELL THAT LABOR IS STARTING?

Labor starts differently for different women. There is no way of telling what they will notice first. (See the descriptions of labor beginning in Question 47.) But a mother often feels a low backache which may circle round to the front. By putting her hand on her abdomen, she can feel the muscles tighten. At first, the contractions may be short and far apart. They may feel like cramps of menstruation. Then, as time passes, they become stronger and closer together. Real labor contractions are regular and rhythmic. But remember, all during pregnancy the uterus has been contracting. Toward the end of pregnancy, these contractions can be felt at odd times and at odd intervals. This is not labor—just practice for labor as the uterus gets ready.

A mother may have other signs of beginning labor,

too. There may be pinkish mucous discharge called "show." This is a sign that the cervix is opening. Sometimes labor is first recognized by a sudden rush of fluid as the bag of water breaks. This isn't usual, but it isn't anything to be troubled about (see Questions 50, 51).

The beginning of labor is a big moment in life, and every woman is naturally excited about it.

46. HOW DO YOU KNOW WHEN TO GO TO THE HOSPITAL?

Before you call the doctor, have ready the answers to the following questions:

Have the membranes ruptured (bag of waters broken)?
What time did the contractions (pains) first begin?
How long do they last?
How strong are they?
How long are the rest periods?
Is there any "show" (red sticky mucus at vagina)?

From the answers to these questions, the doctor will know when to tell you to go to the hospital.

When a mother and father get to the hospital and all preliminaries have been taken care of (see Question 49), the doctor will want to examine his patient. This examination tells him how far along in labor a mother really is. It is not painful if she does not get tense and "tight." His examination is gentle.

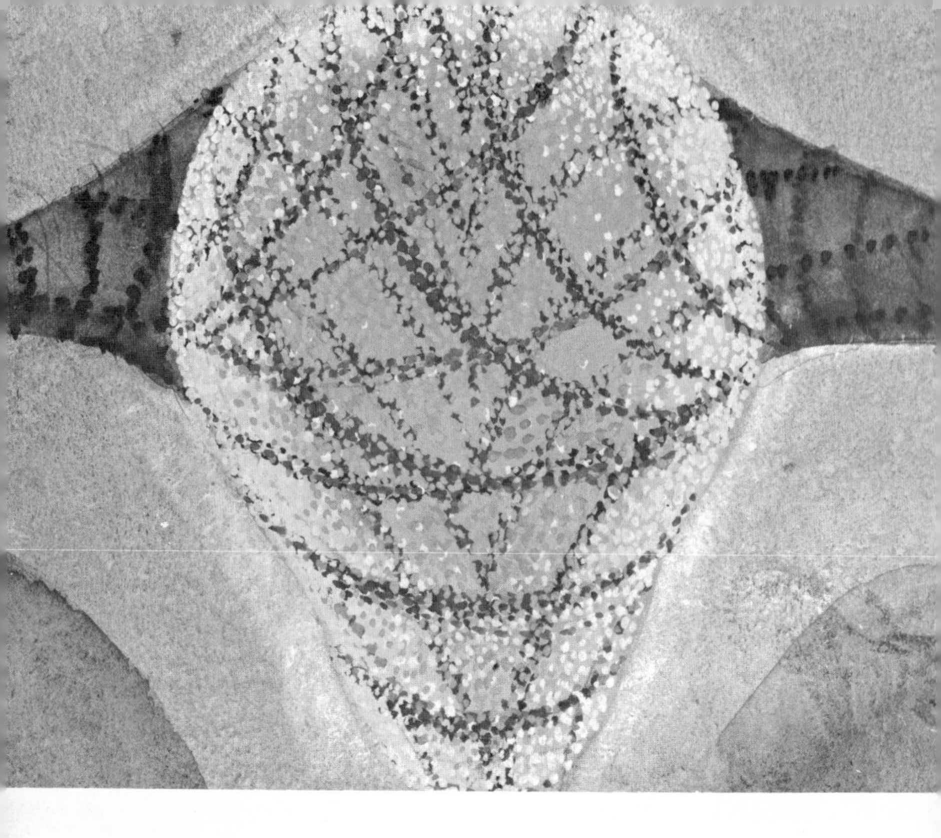

III

About Labor and Birth

47. WHAT IS LABOR? HOW LONG DOES IT LAST?

In labor, the uterus does most of the work. It is composed of layers of muscles (Fig. 58). Some run lengthwise; some circle right to left; some, left to right.

When normal labor begins, these muscles work in harmony to open the uterus and bring the baby into

Fig. 58 (Opposite page) The muscles of the uterus: some run lengthwise; some circle right to left; some left to right.

the world. This alternate tightening and loosening of the muscles is called a contraction. Some people call them "labor pains." Each contraction causes the uterus to get a little smaller.

Labor occurs in three stages.

In the *first stage* of labor, the baby is pressed against the cervix (the opening of the uterus), and little by little this "escape hatch" begins to open (Fig. 59). Progress is slow at first, but as time passes the opening becomes large enough for the baby to come out.

The hours of the first stage may drag. This is when a husband may be of great help. Husbands are good entertainers—talking, playing checkers, doing puzzles or reading poetry. They can remind their wives what to do. And husbands are good back-rubbers and courage bucker-uppers.

Fig. 59 (Below) As labor begins, the first stage is the opening of the cervix.

During the first stage, the mother's job is to relax with the contractions and rest between them. If she begins to get tired, there is always light medication to help her.

Then comes the time of *transition*—six to twelve strong contractions as the muscles of the uterus pull the cervix over the widest part of the baby's head. This may be the most trying part of labor. The mother usually doesn't want to talk at this time. Often she doesn't want anybody to touch her. She may perspire freely, and her body may quiver with the intense activity. Backache may be very strong as the baby's head presses downward. Remind yourself that it lasts for no more than twelve contractions as a rule.

Suddenly the backache passes, and the mother feels that she has to push down. The *second stage* has begun (Fig. 60). This is the time when the mother works hard to push the baby down the birth canal and out into the world. With each contraction, she takes a deep breath, holds it, raises head and legs, and pushes.

Between the contractions, she rests. As the baby's head appears (Fig. 61), the doctor may ask the mother to pant so that the baby may arrive gently. The baby's head is born; this is quickly followed by his shoulders and the rest of his body (Fig. 62).

Sometimes the uterus needs help. The contractions may become weaker or may stop altogether. Then the doctor may give the mother a drug (called an oxytocic) to stimulate the contractions again and hasten the birth of the baby.

The exertion and discomfort may be immediately forgotten in the bringing forth of new life. Hearing the baby's first lusty cry, seeing him squirm in the doctor's or nurse's arms, and then holding him if only for a short time can be a prized experience in life. Many women say that at this time they feel complete.

After the baby is born, the uterus becomes quiet for a short time. Then the contractions begin again, and, in a few minutes, the placenta—which up to now has been the baby's source of oxygen, food and drink—is pushed out. This is the *third stage* of labor (Fig. 63).

No two labors are exactly alike. Sometimes the contractions are long and strong, and the rest periods short. Then again, the contractions may be short and not so strong, and the rest periods long. Sometimes the membranes rupture early; at other times they remain intact until the baby is almost ready to be born. Some babies are large, some are small; some come headfirst, some come in the breech position, bottom-first, or feetfirst (Fig. 64). Some can be moved along the birth canal more readily than others. But the basic process is always the same—the cervix is stretched; then the mother, working with the uterus, pushes the baby out of the uterus, through the birth canal, and into the world.

Fig. 60 (Left) During the second stage, the baby leaves the uterus and is pushed down the birth canal.

Fig. 61 The second stage continues and the baby's head begins to appear. This is called 'crowning.'

Fig. 62 Birth! The baby's head is born. This is quickly followed by his shoulders and the rest of his body.

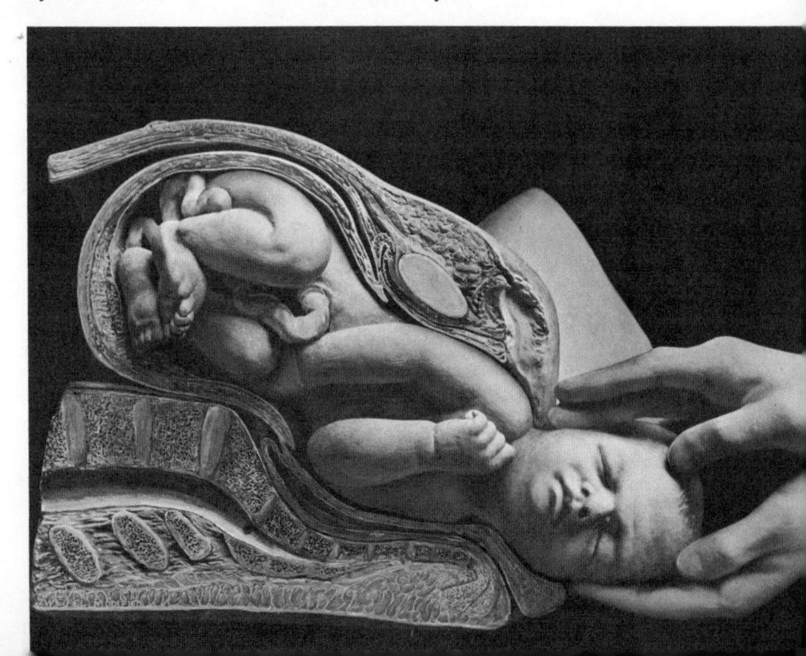

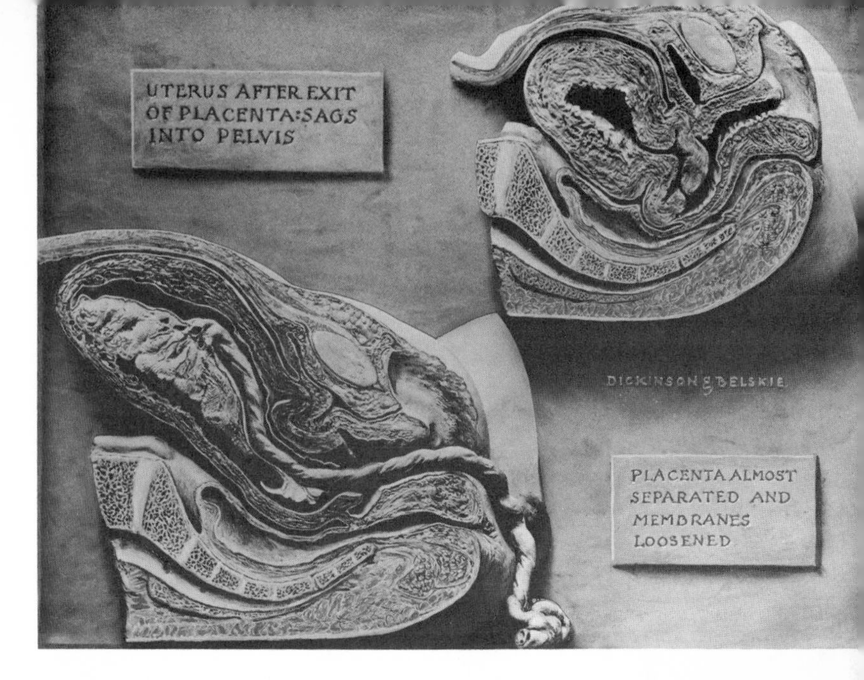

Fig. 63 Third stage: the placenta is expelled.

Fig. 64 Some babies come breech-first.

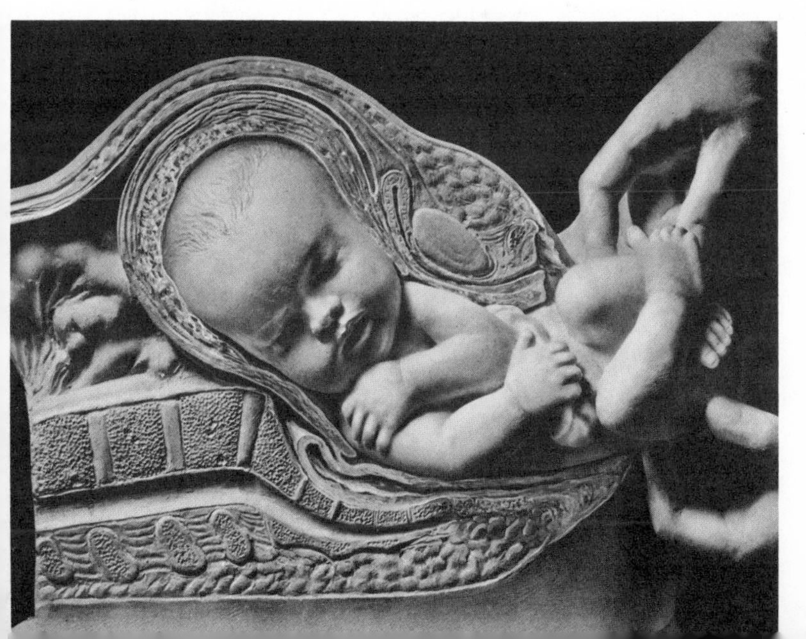

48. WHAT CAUSES LABOR TO BEGIN?

Normal labor begins when the baby is mature enough to live and thrive outside the uterus and small enough to come down the birth canal without causing difficulty to himself or his mother. Medical science does not yet know exactly what causes labor to begin, but there are some theories.

1. Two doctors at the Rockefeller University in New York explain it this way: The uterus is always contracting, whether a woman is pregnant or not. When she becomes pregnant, her ovaries begin to secrete a hormone (progesterone) which keeps the uterus quiet. As the placenta grows, it, too, provides this hormone. So the uterus is kept relatively still and quiet for the months of the baby's growth.

Toward the end of pregnancy, the uterus has grown so rapidly that the hormones secreted by the placenta can no longer keep it still. Little by little the contractions intensify. At first the mother does not feel them. But very late in pregnancy, she becomes conscious of them. These are called Braxton-Hicks contractions—the "setting-up exercises" for labor.

The time comes when the placenta's control over the uterus no longer holds, and the waves of contractions become strong enough to push the baby out. So labor begins!

2. Other scientists think that labor is caused by a body chemical (hormone) called oxytocin which comes from a gland in the brain. As the time of labor draws near, it gives off an increasing amount of oxytocin. When a certain amount of this hormone is in the blood, the uterus is triggered to contract strongly. This is labor.

3. Other doctors think that, when the uterus is

stretched to capacity by the growth of the baby (or babies), it begins its rhythmic contractions to push the baby out.

These are some of the ideas about the causes of labor. Whatever the answer scientifically, perhaps the old saying best explains it: *When the fruit is ripe, it will fall!*

49. WHAT HAPPENS TO THE MOTHER WHEN SHE FIRST GOES TO THE HOSPITAL?

If the mother has never been a patient in a hospital, she may feel strange. Some of the strangeness can be relieved if the mother goes to the hospital before she is in labor and sees the admission desk, the labor room, the delivery room, the nursery, and meets some of the people who will care for her.

A hospital looks forbidding, especially at 3 A.M. Its dark bulk, with only a few lights here and there, does not appear welcoming. But if you know in advance the exact door to use when you enter, you will be more confident when you arrive. In most hospitals, a mother is whisked right off to bed, leaving husband standing in the lobby. If you have secured your doctor's permission to be together during labor, father-to-be will be invited back after you have been "prepped" for labor.

Some hospitals take a medical history at the admission desk. Be patient as the clerk asks all sorts of questions: *Where were you born? Is your mother alive? If not, what did she die of?* and so forth. These questions are asked with a purpose—your protection.

The usual routine is this: first, the mother is asked to undress and put on a hospital gown—one of those strange garments cut "on the half shell"; she is weighed, may be asked for a urine specimen, and most likely put to bed. Temperature, pulse rate and breathing rate will be recorded; a blood sample may be taken. The mother's doctor or the resident physician will examine her, take her blood pressure, feel her abdomen to determine the position and condition of the baby and the strength of the contractions. Through his stethoscope, he will listen to the baby's heartbeat. With his gloved finger, he will also gently examine the birth canal and the cervix (opening of the uterus) to see how far it is dilated and to feel what part of the baby is coming first. A nurse may shave the pubic hair between the mother's legs, and give her a warm enema.

Then the husband, or other companion in labor, will be invited to come in. From time to time, doctor or nurse will examine the mother briefly to see what progress is being made. This will be done in bed. Husband or companion may be asked to step out into the hall while this is taking place.

Often the labor room will have two or four beds in it, with screens between. Then, other women in different stages of labor may be together in the same room.

50. DOES THE BABY COME RIGHT AFTER THE WATER BREAKS?

The sudden gush of water may cause a new mother and father to "push the panic button," and want to hurry off at once to the hospital. There really isn't any need to rush off quickly. The breaking of the bag of waters may be the first sign of beginning labor, with the birth of the baby many hours away. Wait for a short time and see if contractions (pains) begin and if they come regularly. (See Question 46 for the facts to have before you call the doctor.)

Sometimes water gushes out and is not followed by other signs of labor. If this happens, let your doctor know about it.

51. WHAT DOES A "DRY BIRTH" MEAN?

It doesn't mean what many women fear—a harder labor. In fact, there really isn't any such thing as a "dry birth." It is true that the bag of waters does not usually break early in labor, but if it does, only some of the water escapes. The baby's head acts as a stopper, and most of the fluid remains in the uterus. Even if a large proportion of the water drains away, the mother's body continues to produce more.

52. WHAT ABOUT PAIN DURING LABOR?

Many rewarding activities in life have some pain connected with them. Playing strenuous games for fun, or gardening, or any active physical work can leave one with tired and sore muscles. Having a baby is a major job of work requiring the use of many muscles, some of which you seldom use. Very few women go through labor and delivery without some discomfort. The excitement, the straining of muscles, the intense concentration—all these are deeply tiring.

One mother may want to take an active part in the coming of her baby and to cope with pain by learning how to use her natural forces during pregnancy and labor. She wishes to be wide-awake and consciously to push the baby out into the world. She wants to hold her baby as soon as he is born. (See Question 59.)

Another mother prefers to take some drug to avoid the pain and discomfort of having a baby. She does not want to take part in the birth process and prefers to be asleep during the last stages of birth. (See Questions 53–56.)

Talk over your own desires with your doctor early in pregnancy. Tell him what you hope for in labor and delivery. Then put your faith in him. He may have to make a decision during labor that goes against your desires. But he will know what is best at the time and consider the circumstances of your health and the baby's condition in trying to fulfill your hopes.

53. IS THERE A PERFECT DRUG TO RELIEVE PAIN DURING LABOR AND BIRTH?

No, science has not as yet found a perfect analgesic (pain-killer).

But when a mother needs immediate pain relief, the doctor is ready to provide it with one of a number of drugs. Unfortunately, each method or drug for reducing or eliminating pain has some disadvantages. Almost all drugs go into the mother's bloodstream, through the placenta and into the baby's bloodstream. This may affect the baby more deeply than it does the mother. The baby's body is not yet mature enough to rid itself quickly of the drugs after their use is finished. Therefore, the doctor does his best to keep drugs to a minimum—that is, to ease the mother's discomfort without overtaxing the baby with anesthetics.

54. WHAT DRUGS ARE SOMETIMES USED TO REDUCE OR BLOCK OUT PAIN DURING LABOR AND BIRTH?

1. *General anesthetics.* The most widely used drugs

in delivery are nitrous oxide (the laughing gas which the dentist sometimes uses), ether and fluorothane. The mother quickly goes to sleep and has no feeling whatever while her baby is being born. She may have some unpleasant reactions when she is "coming to," but these usually pass in a few hours.

2. *Analgesics.* These are drugs which reduce pain. Sometimes they are combined with drugs which also erase the memory of pain. A person under the effects of this combination may show signs of having pain, but after the event cannot recall any pain at all. Demerol combined with scopolamine is one of the most popular of the combined analgesics given to mothers in labor.

55. WHAT IS A "SPINAL," OR SADDLE BLOCK; A "CAUDAL"; A PUDENDAL BLOCK; A "LOCAL" ANESTHESIA?

1. *Spinal* (saddle block). The doctor injects an anesthetic into the spinal fluid; this blocks feelings in the lower part of the body. The mother remains awake and the baby is not damaged because it does not receive any of the anesthetic through the placenta. Some mothers do not like this because the "block" temporarily numbs the legs and sometimes causes headache after the baby is born.

2. *Caudal.* The anesthetic is injected in the back, close to the spinal canal but not in it. This stops the pain in the nerves but does not affect the muscles of the back and legs. With this method, the doctor often delivers the baby with forceps because the mother has little urge to push.

3. *Pudendal block.* The doctor injects a pain-killing drug through the vagina into the tissues around the

cervix (opening of the uterus) or directly around the larger nerves.

4. *Local anesthesia.* An anesthetic is injected through the opening of the vagina into the nerves around the opening. This numbs the area through which the baby makes his exit, but it does not remove all discomfort. The doctor may also give this mother a few whiffs of gas (nitrous oxide, or "laughing gas"). This further eases her and has almost no aftereffects on mother or baby.

56. HOW ARE TRANQUILIZERS USED IN CHILDBIRTH?

Tranquilizers are drugs which have a calming, relaxing effect. Used with other drugs in labor, they increase the mother's ability to rest and to feel composed.

57. WHAT IS A DELIVERY ROOM LIKE?

For your protection and the baby's, a delivery room is designed for efficiency with few of the things that make other rooms attractive. The doctors and nurses dress in sterile gowns, masks and rubber gloves. Around the room are various appliances to help the mother and the baby if an unexpected emergency arises: a tank of oxygen and a tank of anesthetic gas with a mask, a baby resuscitator and an incubator. There are usually stools for the doctor and anesthetist to sit on, as well as for the husband if he is permitted in the delivery room. There is also a table with instruments and cotton and gauze, usually covered with a towel; a table for examining the baby; and his first crib.

On the wall is a clock to record the exact moment

of the baby's birth. It may also help the mother to time her contractions. A mirror on the wall or overhead makes it possible for the mother to watch the birth of the baby if she wants to see the main event!

In the center of the room is the delivery table, and above it a row of bright lights (Figs. 66 A & B). The mother is wheeled in on her bed or stretcher; or she may walk in. The stirrups on the table are to hold up the mother's legs in comfort so the doctor and nurse can be free to help. The doctor stands or sits at the foot of the table between the mother's legs—watching, coaching and helping the baby to emerge into the world.

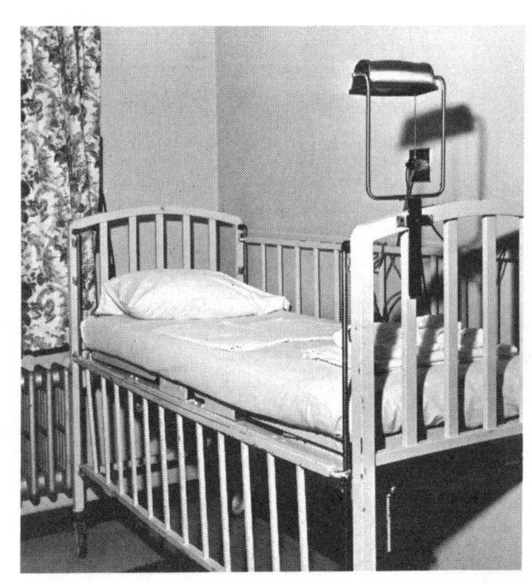

Fig. 65 This is a labor room where the mother stays during the early hours of labor.

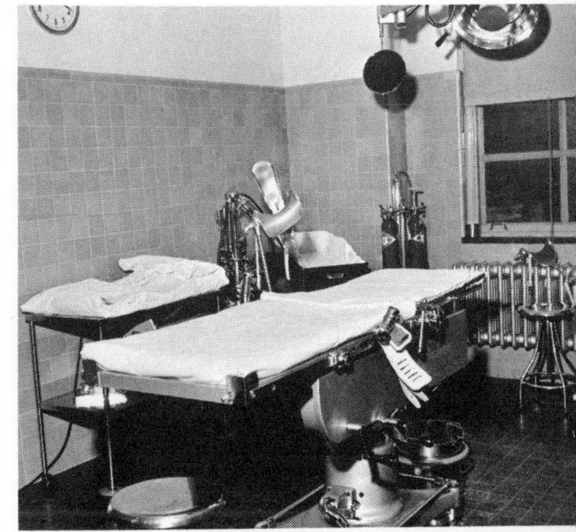

Fig. 66A This is a delivery room all set for the big event.

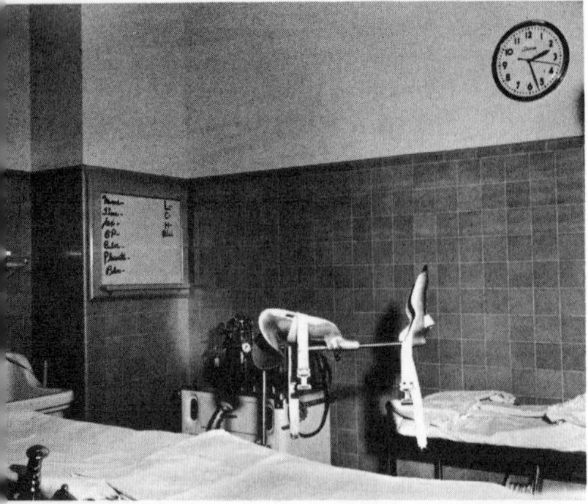

Fig. 66B Another view of the delivery room.

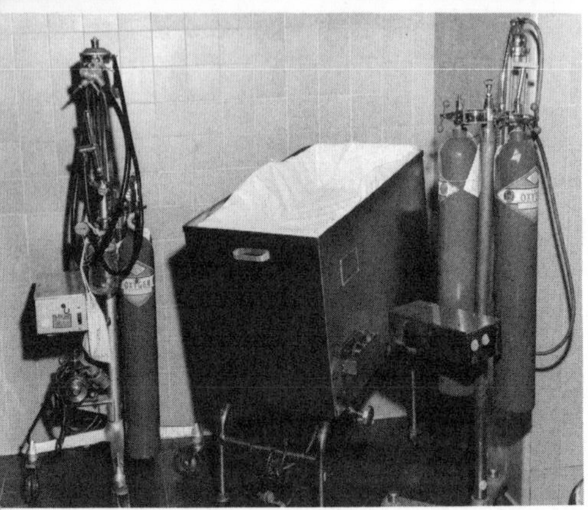

Fig. 67 This is baby's first bed with everything ready to help him take his first breath.

The delivery position can be tiring because the mother must keep her legs wide apart for about twenty minutes. Muscles can be trained for this during pregnancy by practicing the position shown in Figure 68.

Fig. 68 Mother readies herself for delivery.

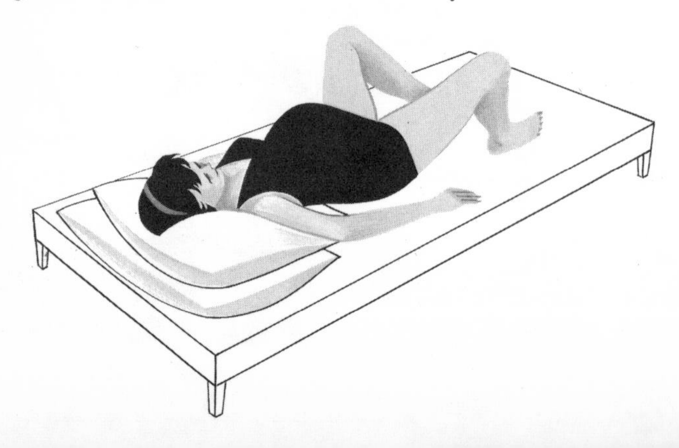

58. DO ALL WOMEN NEED STITCHES AFTER DELIVERY?

No, but as the baby's head is being born, usually the doctor makes a surgical cut, under anesthesia, in the muscle wall of the perineum (the bridge of tissue between the vagina and the anus). This cut is called an *episiotomy*. The doctor does this to avoid a possible irregular tear from the pressure of the baby's oncoming head. An episiotomy may also help to strengthen the tissues of the perineum so that, during later life, the chances of difficulty in these tissues due to childbearing are lessened.

After the baby is born, the doctor takes a few stitches to close this cut. Women in the past have talked so much about stitches because they are in a sensitive place and often caused some discomfort. But today the repair is so much more refined that women are often unaware that they have had stitches.

59. HOW CAN "NATURAL CHILDBIRTH" OR "PSYCHOPROPHYLAXIS" HELP A MOTHER IN CHILDBEARING?

A mother may feel very strongly, "I want to have a part in the birth of my baby," or "I want to be awake when our baby is born." She may not want to be "knocked out" when she is ready to give birth. Parents who feel this way often go to classes to learn what to expect during pregnancy and labor, how they can best help themselves at each point, and what help they can expect from doctors and nurses.

According to Dr. Grantly Dick Read, an English doctor who wrote a very popular book, *Childbirth*

Without Fear, birth does not have to be unbearably painful. Pain, he said, is caused by tension, and tension by fear. Women fear childbearing, he wrote, because they do not know what is ahead during the nine months of pregnancy and the hours of labor. They may have heard their own mothers and friends tell stories of frightful times in labor and wonder if it will be the same for them.

Because of these "old wives' tales," many women think of labor as a time of increasing pain until the baby is born. If they are uncomfortable at the end of a few hours of labor, they look to the hours ahead with fear and trembling. They do not know that the discomforts of labor do not necessarily increase steadily.

There often is discomfort during the early hours and it may intensify during the time between the first and second stages of labor (see Question 47). This is when the cervix opens wide enough to permit the baby to enter the lower birth canal. After this happens, the mother feels like pushing; and pushing is usually not painful.

By attending classes during pregnancy, many parents lose these fears of childbirth and are better able to enjoy being pregnant. The woman learns how to walk, sit, stand and lie down comfortably as the baby grows bigger. She learns how proper breathing promotes relaxation so she can reduce the tension in her muscles. This will help to prevent pain in labor.

Doctors have also learned that feelings of pain can be blocked by the power of suggestion called "conditioning." In this approach to childbirth, known as psychoprophylaxis, mothers also learn exercises and breathing patterns for labor. Most women in France and the Soviet Union have their babies by this method, and its use is growing throughout the world.

As one Russian doctor writes: "It requires a lot of effort and trouble on the part of doctors and midwives. But the joy and happiness of the mother, who gives birth to a healthy child without pain, fear and complications . . . fully compensate for the difficulties of the method and give great satisfaction to all."

A mother doesn't really succeed or fail in any of these "natural childbirth" methods. Each mother goes as far as she feels she is able. She can ask for anesthetic help at any time. Each person reacts differently to pain. Some feel discomfort or pain more intensely than others. No mother who has her baby by any of these methods has failed if she needs drugs at some point in labor. She has helped herself and has protected her baby from unnecessary or large amounts of drugs.

Sometimes a mother who wants to have her baby by one of these methods comes into a hospital in labor calm and completely self-controlled. As labor progresses, she will need someone to help her to apply what she has learned and to encourage her efforts. Husbands who have learned what to expect hour by hour can be of great help if the hospital will let them stay with their wives. Some women don't want to have their husbands with them; some husbands don't want to be there. But no woman wants to be alone during labor. The companion could be mother or mother-in-law, sister or friend, nurse or doctor. That somebody, however, should be able to help the mother to relax during contractions —rubbing her back when it is uncomfortable and generally being a good companion.

Dr. C. Lee Buxton, former professor of obstetrics and gynecology at Yale, recently studied the methods of psychophysical relief of pain in this country and Europe. He found that eight out of ten mothers in the centers he visited suffered no pain or had pain which they could easily bear.

If you are interested in having your baby by one of these methods, talk it over with your doctor the first time you visit him. Find out if he is interested in working with you. He may offer special classes for the instruction of mothers and fathers, or he may refer you to a hospital or other community agency such as a visiting nurse association. In many cities, special groups of parents have been organized to help prepare mothers for childbearing. They go under such names as: Childhood-Parenthood Association; Childbirth Education Association; Parent-Child, Inc.; Parentcraft Center; etc. If you cannot find such an organization in your community, write to the International Childbirth Education Association, 1310 North 26th Street, Milwaukee, Wisc. 53205, to find out if there is such an organization near you.

Maternity Center Association, 48 East 92nd Street, New York, N. Y. 10028, publishes a booklet, "Preparation for Childbearing" ($1.00), containing instructions on breathing, relaxation and exercises. Practice of these exercises should be regular and consistent; twenty minutes a day should be adequate. With conscientious practice—if your doctor agrees that this is for you—you should look better, feel better, and look forward to labor, confident that you can help yourself and cooperate better with the doctors and nurses who help you.

Suggested reading:

Childbirth Without Fear. Dr. Grantly Dick Read. New York, Harper & Row, $3.00.

Childbirth Without Pain. Dr. Pierre Vellay. New York, Dutton. $4.95.

Preparing for Childbirth. Dr. Frederick W. Goodrich, Jr. Englewood Cliffs, N.J., Prentice-Hall. $4.95.

60. HOW IS HYPNOSIS USED IN CHILDBIRTH?

Hypnosis is an approach to childbirth which has recently been recognized by the American Medical Association as an acceptable medical procedure. It requires a doctor specially trained in the art. It is easy to hypnotize a person, but not all women can benefit from this method. The doctor, therefore, must select carefully who is to be hypnotized.

Under the right conditions, hypnosis can be very successful. Dr. William E. F. Werner describes an ideal situation in the *New York State Journal of Medicine:*

> In an anteroom just off the maternity suite in a hospital sits a mother in labor. Her contractions started about two hours ago at home, and she came to the hospital at once. . . . Now she sits in a comfortable chair with her husband at her side. With each contraction she puts herself into a deep hypnotic trance [which the doctor taught her how to do during pregnancy] and remains in the trance while the contraction lasts. Then she opens her eyes; she appears completely refreshed and joins in whatever activities are taking place in the room at the time. She may eat or drink.
>
> After an hour or two, she tells the person standing by that she feels like pushing or bearing down. The doctor is called, and she is immediately taken to the delivery room. With each contraction, she works hard—bearing down without any coaxing by doctor or nurse. She is reminded that she will be rewarded for her hard work with a tremendous sense of well-being. After some fifteen or twenty minutes, she has her baby. She is then awakened to see her baby and to hear his first cry. . . .

This sounds ideal, and for some it is. But only certain women can be deeply hypnotized. Others may go into a light trance and be in perfect control for many hours. Then at the last they may need some drug to help them over the most important, final moments of birth.

61. SHOULD HUSBANDS BE WITH THEIR WIVES IN THE DELIVERY ROOM?

The question of husband in the delivery room has been debated for several years. In some states he has been legally barred as a nonessential person. The reasons given were that he might "get in the way," "become faint," or "contaminate the delivery room." Some hospital administrators have ruled against it to protect him from witnessing unforeseen complications.

This opposition is still strong in some communities. Many husbands and wives don't want to be together. But fathers are being admitted to a growing number of hospital delivery rooms. Dr. Robert A. Bradley, at Porter Hospital in Denver, has had nearly ten years' experience of admitting fathers, and he feels that it is an "exhilarating experience for the parents, advantageous to the hospital and a useful practice for the obstetrician."

Dr. Bradley believes that, before a father is admitted to a delivery room, both he and his wife should be prepared for this experience in special classes. He also feels that the father should really want to be there. This does not mean that every man who looks squeamish at the first mention of the idea should be immediately excluded. Dr. Bradley says that at Porter Hospital probably seventy-five percent of the husbands look on the idea skeptically at first. But when it is explained to them why they should be there, and how they can help their

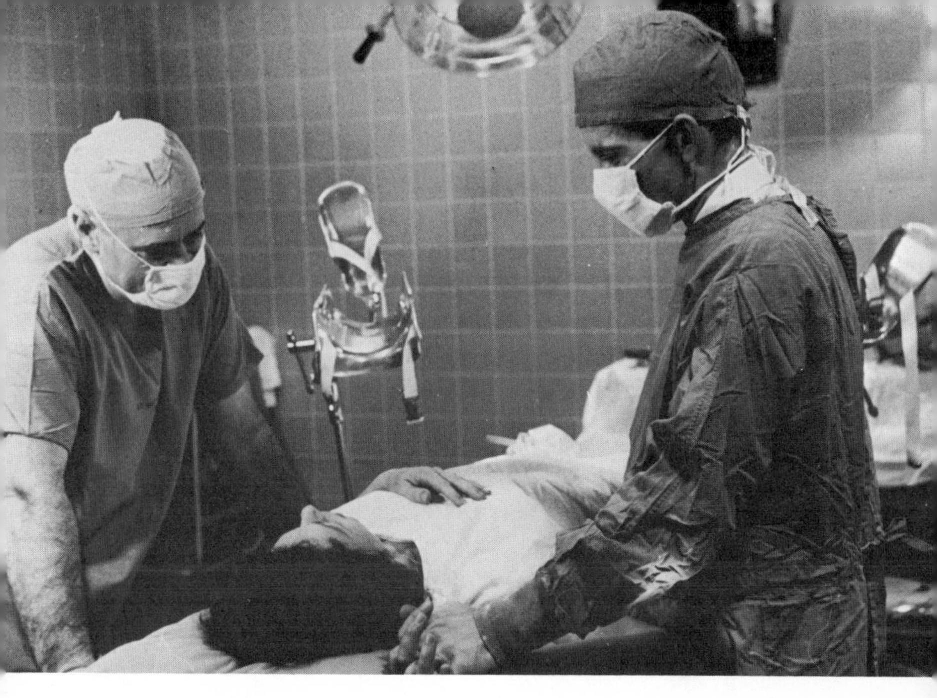

Fig. 69 Father (right) in delivery room. From St. Mary's Hospital, Evansville, Indiana.

wives during the important moments of birth, over ninety-five percent change their minds and are enthusiastic afterwards (Fig. 69).

62. WHAT IS "FAMILY-CENTERED" CARE IN A HOSPITAL?

Family-centered care is based on the idea that families belong together at the time the new baby arrives. Every effort is made to create a relaxed, homelike atmosphere for the whole family—mother, father and baby.

Teaching is an important part of family-centered hospital care. When a mother and baby are discharged from the hospital, the mother and father have a knowledge and understanding about their baby and themselves which can give them a feeling of confidence.

At St. Mary's Hospital in Evansville, Indiana, for instance, when a mother is admitted in labor, she and her husband go directly to the labor room. While the mother is being "prepped," the husband returns to the admitting desk to fill out the forms and answer the questions. The mother in labor is spared all the paperwork.

At no time in labor is the mother left alone. She receives support and encouragement from her husband (who stays with her), her doctor and the hospital nurses and aides. When ready to be delivered, she is taken to the delivery room, accompanied by her husband; or, if they do not wish to be together at that time, the husband is provided with comfortable quarters just outside.

After the baby is born, the mother, father and baby go to the recovery room where the mother and baby are closely observed for about eight hours. From the beginning, the mother is taught to care for herself and her baby. The father may hold the baby at this time, and is shown the importance of washing his hands and putting on a gown.

Fig. 70 At St. Mary's Hospital mothers learn baby care in a friendly atmosphere.

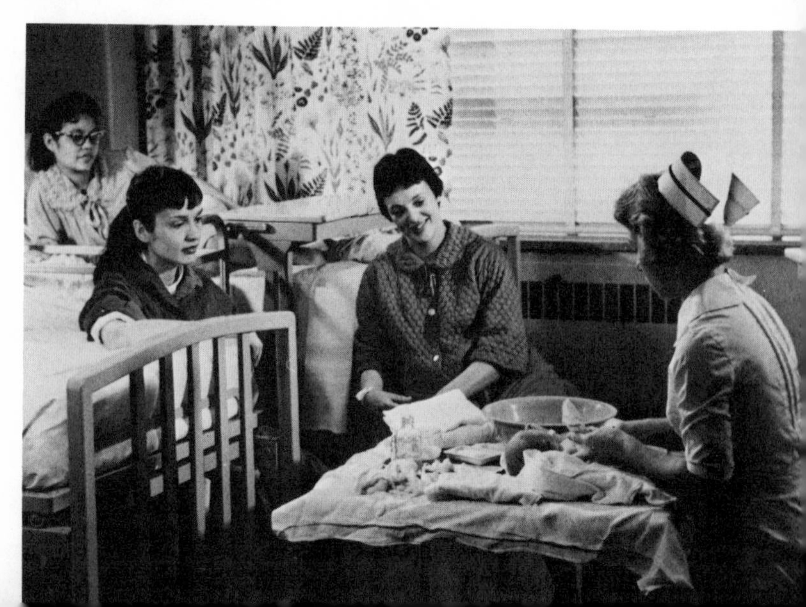

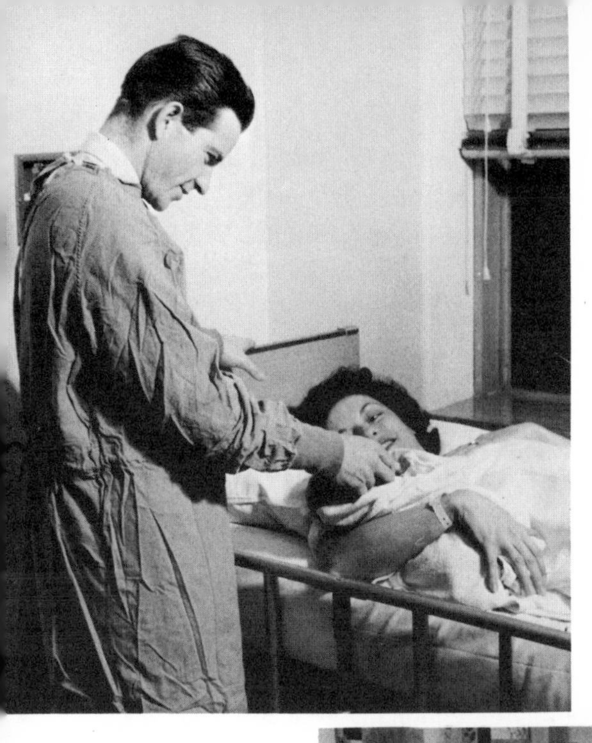

Fig. 71 Father gets acquainted in the recovery room.

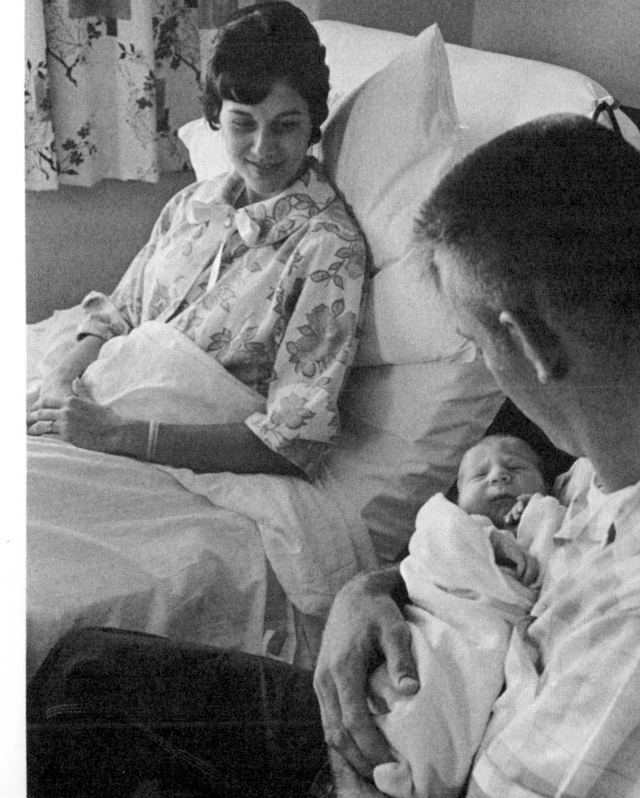

Fig. 72 Maternity care is family-centered.

After the eight-hour observation period, the mother is given the type of room accommodation she booked in advance. She may care for her baby as much or as little as she wishes. When not at the mother's bedside, the baby is kept in a small nursery while in the hospital.

During visiting hours, the baby must remain in the nursery. At all other times, the husband may visit and, after proper preparation, may handle the baby. At night, the baby is kept in the nursery under the care of a nurse's aide, unless the mother prefers having the baby with her. The baby is on demand-feeding—that is, he is fed whenever he is hungry. Breast-feeding is encouraged; but the mother is supplied with formula when needed, or she may request the nurse or nurse's aide to feed the baby.

Dr. Edgar L. Engel of St. Mary's Hospital says that the maternity floor is exceptionally peaceful and quiet because:

> when the infant is near the mother, it receives personal, full-time observation and attention. When it cries, the mother takes care of it. If the baby has a wet diaper, it can be changed immediately and as a consequence there is very little diaper rash. When the baby is hungry, it can be fed on demand. On the other hand, in a central nursery there is comparatively less opportunity for personal attention. Noise is generally at a far higher level, particularly in the half hour prior to feeding schedule.

A number of hospitals all across the country provide this friendly, warm maternity care. A few provide care on an "assembly-line." Most hospitals fall in between these two extremes. What kind of care do you want? Ask about it while you are pregnant, so you won't be disappointed when you have your baby in the hospital.

63. WHAT IS IT REALLY LIKE TO GIVE BIRTH?

Three Birth Experiences

These are excerpts from three letters sent to Maternity Center Association by mothers who had attended classes for expectant parents. The letters illustrate the fact that normal labor and delivery can be very different for different women. But throughout all the hundreds of letters from new mothers received at the Center, one finds the same feeling of achievement and excitement. There may have been some tense moments (as in all important life experiences), but the reward is great.

It's a Girl!

Dear M.C.A.:

It's a girl! All the infallible sources (mother-in-law, sisters-in-law, girl friends, doctor's nurse, etc., etc) had predicted it would be a boy and they had me nearly convinced. When the doctor said, "It's a girl!" as he held her up, I did a triple-take. Clearly he was right.

Our daughter, Judy, arrived at 11:22 A.M. Thursday, after a long labor, and a quick, easy delivery. She weighed in at six pounds, eight ounces, and came complete with reddish-brown hair, blue eyes, and long eyelashes. She looked feminine from the start and has gotten more so every day. It's clear she'll be beautiful, but I'm a little afraid she'll turn out to be a beautiful female wrestler. She held her head up by Friday A.M. and when papa put her down on her back Friday night, she gave him a *look,* and promptly pushed herself over onto her side.

I was blessed with a marvelous nurse and doctor, but it was my husband who really saw me through. . . . Please teach fathers how to really bear down hard on aching backs! For me, it made the difference between misery and tenseness and mild discomfort with catnaps between contractions. The nurse came in when he went off for breakfast, but it wasn't the same. I was about ready for a general anesthetic by the time he got back and leveled me off again! I was awfully glad I had seen it through without a general anesthetic! A few hours later in the delivery room I was awake and saw Judy dangling by her ankles, gathering breath for her first howl. They brought her to me in the recovery room a very short time later, unwashed but unbelievably cuddlesome. My husband joined us a little later and they let the three of us visit for a good half-hour. (The sign said only ten minutes, but . . .!) In fact, the doctor wouldn't tell him if it was a girl or a boy—just sent him in to ask me. I assumed he knew and my "Come meet your daughter" was pretty off-hand.

To be more specific about the medical details, I never had a surge of energy or the other usual warning signs of the coming of labor. Wednesday morning I woke, dripping. The bag of waters had ruptured some and I had some "show." I let the doctor know and settled down to await contractions. Actually I felt very tired and slightly nauseous, so I hoped this was the beginning. I napped and felt better. Maybe once an hour or so, I'd have a noticeable contraction and a gusher from the amniotic sac. I was afraid to go out because of that. By three P.M. I was very restless and hadn't gushed in a while so I went out for a walk with husband and dog. Just restless waiting around describes the day. The doctor called to check and said just liquids for supper.

I was having sporadic mild contractions from five to six P.M. By seven P.M. they settled into ten-minute intervals. By 7:45 I gave Bill the stopwatch so I couldn't cheat. By 8:30 mild contractions had been seven minutes apart for over an hour, so we called the doctor and slowly collected ourselves for the hospital. (The suitcase had been ready for weeks.) As we left the house, my knees started shaking; suddenly we were both nervous wrecks!

I got to the hospital about ten P.M. and was "prepped" by an angelic nurse who had great understanding of my butterflies. Bill joined me toward 11. We timed the contractions—five minutes apart. When the doctor came he felt it would be some hours, assured us we could call him if we felt need and the nurse would call when there was need. He went off to sleep down the hall.

My tale now gets hazy. I found I was most comfortable on my side, both legs bent. I felt my contractions almost entirely in my back. I began to doze between contractions, and Bill followed suit. The next thing I knew, the doctor was back to check. We didn't even have a time check for him, but it turned out they were four minutes apart and I was far from ready. The doctor went back to bed. Bill carried me along—back rubs, shoulder rubs, words of cheer. I kept thinking I *must* send him home to get some rest.

Toward eight A.M. the doctor checked again, and said OK, I can start to push (second stage). That was music to my ears because I had had a strong urge to push for ages. In the delivery room the doctor showed me how to use the hand grips (on the delivery table) and got me all set to push while he washed up. Then he gave me a pudendal block [see Question 55]. He did it while I was pushing. I felt three pin pricks. Another pin prick for the episiotomy [see Question 58] and the next moment there was Judy! I was too busy watching her get her eye drops, wiggle, and howl to notice much. Out came the placenta, then the stitches, and off to "recovery."

The head nursery nurse helped me with nursing every feeding. I learned the problem is that the baby isn't *that* hungry, and it takes three hands at first! Judy's appetite appeared on Sunday, and my milk soon after. Now, it's smooth sailing. Tomorrow we go home!

False Alarm

Dear M.C.A.:

Our baby was born two weeks ago today at 11:59 P.M. and weighed seven pounds, 11 ounces. (My doctor predicted he would be six days late, which he was with one minute to spare!) It seems so long ago that I was pregnant, although I must say those last few weeks seemed like eternity.

We had a false alarm three days before he was born, and I'm sure I would think I was in labor if the same things happened again. . . . On Sunday at 6:30 P.M. I had a "show" of blood. All excited, I called the doctor who told me to call back when the contractions were ten minutes apart. There weren't any until midnight, and then I had one-and-one-half hours of the kind that were described in class—from six to eight minutes apart and lasting about forty seconds each. I was finding shallow breathing very helpful at that point.

The doctor asked me to go to the hospital. We were very well organized and calm, and I kept saying "I'm not *really* having a baby, am I?" I arrived at the hospital at 3:30 A.M. and was all prepared, enema, shave, etc. At 6:30 the contractions stopped and at noon John took me home—and I was very frustrated!

On Wednesday morning, therefore, when I started to leak gushes of water, I was determined not to make a mistake again. I had no pains until 9 A.M., by which time my contractions were about ten minutes apart, 30 seconds long, and each accompanied by a leak of water and a little blood. (Incidentally, I recommend a sheet of plastic over the mattress and under the sheet for those last two weeks. I did this and I'm sure it saved my mattress.)

The doctor scolded me for waiting so long, and told me to come to the hospital again. I called John, who was even calmer this time after our "dress rehearsal," and was all packed when he came to get me. It took us one-half hour to get to the hospital and my pains increased in frequency and severity. We finally realized that this was IT.

I was admitted to the hospital at one P.M. and, all in all, had 15 hours of labor. I suppose this is average, but it seemed like forever to me. John was with me from the time we got to the hospital until midnight when the baby was born. We both saw him come out and heard his first cry. This was worth everything! John was marvelous—patient and calm—and above all, he was *there.* Knowing this made it easier for me.

I was given demerol at about eight P.M., and at first it helped, but didn't seem to later on. I had a shot of scopolamine at about 10 P.M., but although my thoughts wandered a bit, I was fully conscious of everything and everyone.

John, Jr., came out without any forceps needed and without a mark on him. I definitely recommend that a woman have her husband with her if she can, and if he wants to be there. It is a wonderful experience which cannot be described.

Labor Can Be Short and Intense

Dear M.C.A.:

My labor began (to my knowledge) about 3:30 A.M. We left for the hospital at five A.M., arriving at six A.M. I was prepared and transferred to the labor room at about 6:30 A.M.; transferred to the delivery room minutes later, and baby arrived at 7:04 A.M. The transition phase (from first to second stage of labor) was unpleasant as I had chills and shook all over. This made the process of dressing and getting to the hospital difficult, plus the fact that contractions were every three minutes.

On arrival at the hospital, I had about two double contractions and then had the desire to push while en route to labor-delivery floor. However, once in the labor room, I was told I was already in the second stage and could push. At once I felt relieved. Second-stage labor was not in the least unpleasant. I can't recall the total number of pushes it took for the head to come, but it didn't seem very many at all. It was exciting! The mirror [on the wall of the delivery room] was adjusted so I could watch. The anesthetist sat alongside and reminded me to look when the head and shoulders presented.

The baby was blue only momentarily and then I saw him turn pink. His eyes were open and he was soon making little sucking noises. He was very alert from the first cry. Third stage was less pleasant [expulsion of the placenta] as the massaging of my abdomen hurt, and I winced a bit as a couple of stitches were taken.

During recovery period I rested but actually did not feel very tired as my labor had been so short. I just felt very pleased. I could hear the baby sucking away on the other side of the room (not very far from me). Once back in my room, I dropped off to sleep after seeing my husband. I slept from nine to 12. At noon I felt hungry enough to eat every bit of food on my tray—and I did!

As my doctor said, I had a labor and delivery which was definitely not average for first baby. When my labor first became apparent to me, I thought I was in false labor because the contractions were somewhat irregular. The contractions were very hard and it was difficult for me to time them. I had my husband time the contractions and call the doctor as I didn't feel capable of doing anything much at that point. Had it not been for my husband's insistence that we go to the hospital, I might have had my baby at home.

64. WHAT IS A BREECH BIRTH?

Babies are born in different positions. Most come headfirst (the vertex position). But four out of a hundred come bottom-first or feetfirst. This is called the breech position. It is normal, but it requires the skillful care of an experienced doctor (Figs. 73 and 74).

When the baby comes headfirst, his breathing can begin as soon as his head is born. Sometimes a baby cries (taking in life-giving oxygen) as soon as his head comes out. In breech birth, the baby's nose and mouth are the last to be born.

Just what causes a breech birth is not fully known, but if your baby's position is breech, don't be anxious. You have chosen your doctor because you have confidence in him. Trust him now! He will know whether the baby will fit through the birth canal in any position.

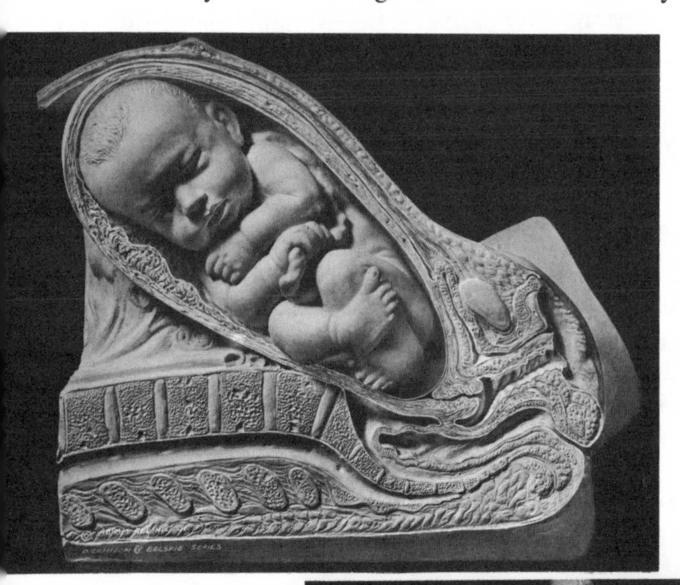

Fig. 73 The breech position—just before labor begins.

Fig. 74 The doctor may straddle the baby's body across his arm and gently put pressure on the mother's abdomen. This quickly pushes the baby's head out.

65 WHY ARE SOME BABIES "INSTRUMENT BABIES"?

Sometimes the mother or baby may need extra help. The mother may become tired. Or her uterus may not be pushing the baby out efficiently. Or the drugs used to reduce her discomfort may sometimes reduce the strength of the contractions. The doctor may decide that the baby would be better off if he were born sooner. Or perhaps the size of the baby's head does not exactly match the size of the mother's pelvis, and the baby needs a little help to get through.

This is when the doctor may use "instruments" or forceps.

Forceps are marvelously constructed metal blades which the doctor fits, one at a time, around the baby's head. Then he locks them together at their handles and is able to ease the baby's head out by gently pulling on the handles as the uterus pushes from above.

The mother and father should not be disturbed if the baby has red marks on his head and face caused by the blades of the forceps. These marks will disappear in a day or two.

66. WHAT IS A CESAREAN?

A cesarean section is an abdominal operation. The mother is completely anesthetized, and the baby is taken through the walls of the abdomen and the uterus. In the past, a cesarean was very risky for mother and baby, but modern medical science has made it much safer. For certain mothers it may be far safer to have their babies by cesarean than by normal delivery. However, it must be remembered that a cesarean is still an abdominal operation with the risks of a surgical procedure. A doctor doesn't do a cesarean just because a mother wants to escape the hours of normal labor. Sometimes a mother, in fear of the pains of labor, forgets that the recovery from a cesarean operation also has its discomforts. Usually the doctor consults with other doctors before he makes a decision to remove the baby from the uterus by cesarean.

Why is a cesarean sometimes recommended—even to a mother who has been looking forward to her birth experience? Among the chief reasons are:

(1) *Disproportion*—that is, the baby is too big for the exit. If a mother has diabetes, for instance, her pelvis may be normal but her baby may be much larger than average. Or a mother may have a pelvis with a small outlet.

(2) The mother has been in labor, but *progress is too slow;* her uterus is not working efficiently, and the baby shows signs of distress.

(3) *The placenta (afterbirth) has grown across the cervix* (mouth of the uterus), blocking the baby's exit.

(4) *The baby may lie crosswise in the uterus (the transverse position).*

(5) *Rh difficulties.* (See Question 36.)

Once a cesarean, always a cesarean was a medical axiom for years, but not so today. A study was made in a big New York hospital a few years ago which indicates that over half of the mothers who had had one cesarean had their later babies safely and successfully in the usual manner. The doctors doing the study added, "*Once a cesarean, always a cesarean* does not apply to current practice. Rather, the management of each patient should be individualized."

67. CAN MOTHERS HAVE THEIR BABIES "BY APPOINTMENT"?

Some women like the idea of setting the time for the baby's birthday in advance, going to the hospital, and having the doctor start labor with powerful drugs called oxytocics. Most doctors avoid the induction of labor unless special conditions call for it. For mothers who live a long distance from the hospital, for instance, the worry about getting there in time is eliminated, especially in the winter when the roads may be blocked by ice and snow. Sometimes the doctor may feel that the mother's physical or emotional condition calls for an induced labor. But, as Dr. George Schaefer of New York-Cornell Medical Center warns, "Elective induction requires special doctors, special equipment, and constant attention."

IV

After the Baby Comes

In the Hospital

68. HOW IS THE MOTHER LIKELY TO FEEL AFTER THE BABY IS BORN?

After the baby is born and you have enjoyed with your husband the wonderful moment of meeting the new member of your family, you may suddenly feel very weary while still feeling "on top of the world." Your uterus will also remind you of the now-finished exertions of labor by contracting from time to time. Some of these contractions may be uncomfortable.

You may be ravenously hungry and thirsty. You may eat what you want—unless your doctor has restricted your diet. Drink lots of liquids. This will help you over this time of weariness. Don't lie still—move around in bed, stretching from head to toe (see Question 19).

On the first day after the baby is born, just be lazy and relaxed. Your doctor will probably let you dangle your legs over the side of the bed and walk to the bathroom whenever you wish.

Those loving visitors! Their intentions are good but they can be so tiring! Don't let them get you down. Politely let them know when you've had enough. Perhaps your husband can speak to them beforehand so they won't stay too long.

Your muscles may be sore. You have been exercising many different muscles in your back, shoulders and arms—even in your hands, legs and abdomen. So be prepared to feel as if you had bowled for the first time.

In the next days, you will feel stronger and may be allowed to get out of bed whenever you wish. But don't overdo it. Remember, the first few days at home are going to be strenuous—bringing baby home, organizing your housework and your lives to include the baby and his needs. So take it easy while you can.

About the third day, the milk comes into your breasts. They may become hard and tender to the touch. If you plan to bottle-feed the baby, the doctor will give you something to stop the flow of milk.

Between the third and fifth days, a few mothers (fewer than one out of ten) experience a letdown called *baby blues.* They may cry, but laugh through their tears. The experts believe that this mixed-up feeling is caused by a change in the body's chemistry after having the baby. It may also be a reaction to the sudden end of the excitement. The visitors have come and gone, and the responsibilities for the baby begin to loom larger. Once in a while, this feeling gets delayed, and suddenly hits you after you've been home a day or two. For those few who have baby blues, the feeling passes quickly. The next day you'll wonder why you were upset at all!

Some mothers leave the hospital after the third day. Stay a few more days if it is at all possible. You may still be tired and just beginning to learn what the new baby is like and how to care for him.

Six Weeks' Check-Up

Your need for the doctor's care doesn't end when you take the baby from the hospital. Make a note to plan a return visit to the doctor or clinic about six weeks after the baby comes. (Of course, if you have questions or problems in the meantime, use the telephone.) The six weeks' check-up is very important to your future health —the doctor wants to make sure that your body has readjusted to becoming *not* pregnant.

69. WHAT ABOUT KEEPING THE BABY IN THE MOTHER'S ROOM IN THE HOSPITAL (ROOMING-IN)?

Recent studies by doctors and psychologists show that there may be a relation between the kind of care a newborn baby gets and the kind of person he grows up to be. These experts look with friendly eye on rooming-in in modern hospitals where mother and baby can be together, getting to know each other.

Rooming-in offers many advantages. Mothers can pick up their babies and cuddle them whenever they wish. If a woman is tired and wants to doze or daydream, the nurses care for the baby. Before going home, the baby

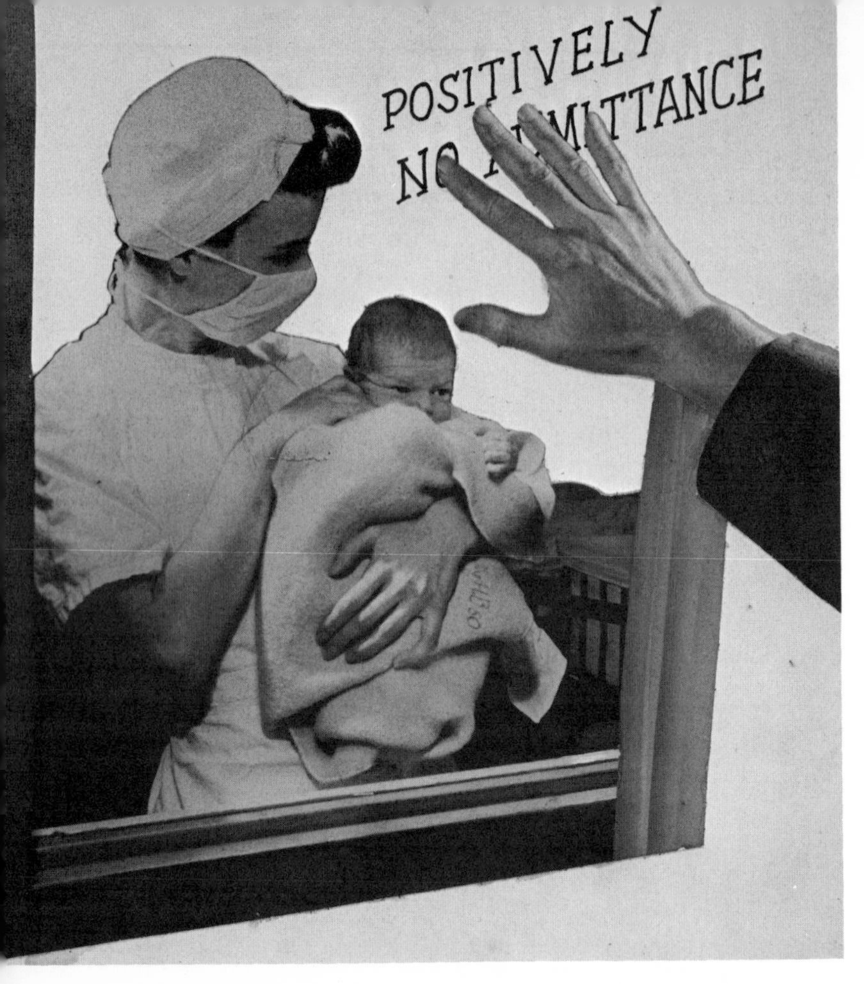

Fig. 75 A wall of frustration.

gets accustomed to his mother's voice and the touch of her hands. She also knows what his cries or snuffling mean. This should make the change from hospital to home much easier for mother and baby because each feels secure with the other.

By rooming-in, the mother can feed her baby when he wants to be fed rather than following a hospital schedule that may not suit his appetite. This can be very important if the mother plans to nurse her baby, for this is a time of testing for both with helpful nurses close at hand.

Husbands often like it better, too. A father gets a chance to hold and care for his baby instead of an unsatisfactory peek through the nursery window (Fig. 75). He usually wears a gown when he enters the room. Of course, he washes his hands. Other visitors, including family members, may be limited in some rooming-in units.

If *you* want rooming-in arrangements, ask your doctor if the hospital to which he plans to take you is equipped to provide this kind of care.

70. WHAT ABOUT KEEPING THE BABY IN A CENTRAL NURSERY IN THE HOSPITAL?

Some hospitals do not have rooming-in facilities and must care for babies in central nurseries. The nurses or aides change the baby and talk to him, and feed him at night if the mother is not breast-feeding.

The baby is brought to the mother on a hospital schedule for feeding or for a brief "hello." She won't get a chance to practice baby-care skills or to strike up a lengthy conversation. But the days pass quickly, and soon he is home with his mother and father.

71. WHAT IS PKU, AND WHY SHOULD BABIES BE TESTED FOR IT SOON AFTER BIRTH?

PKU—an inherited condition with a long name, phenylketonuria—is a very rare disease (one case out of 20,000 births) which, if untreated, can cause mental retardation. It is due to the baby's inability to make use of a certain part of his food—a protein, phenylalanine. This can damage his brain.

To test for PKU, the doctor takes a tiny sample of the baby's heel blood while he's still in the hospital. Sometimes the parents are given small pieces of chemically treated paper to test the baby's urine at home. They put a piece in his diaper a week or two after homecoming, sending it back to the hospital for tests.

If the tests show that the baby has PKU, the doctor prescribes a special diet. Usually, the baby, fed on this diet, grows up to be a strong, healthy child.

72. WHY ARE SOME BABIES BORN TOO SOON (PREMATURE BABIES)?

Science does not know all the answers, but it seems to be a fact that people who live at a low level of income—with poor diet, poor housing, and general insecurity—have more premature babies than those who are more fortunate. "Preemies," however, are born to mothers from all socioeconomic levels.

Prematurity may be due to a hidden infection, or to a placenta which is not well rooted in the uterus, or to *toxemia,* a condition with high blood pressure and poorly working kidneys. Early, continuous medical care in pregnancy can do much to prevent and control toxemia.

73 HOW MAY PREMATURE BABIES DIFFER FROM FULL-TERM (NINE-MONTH) BABIES?

A baby who weighs less than 5½ pounds at birth usually needs special premature care (see Question 75), whether or not he is born before the end of nine months. Some small parents, however, may have five-pound babies who are ready for life outside the uterus, and therefore would not be considered premature.

A premature baby is thin and red, often looking like a tiny, wrinkled old man or woman.

74. DO SEVEN-MONTH BABIES HAVE A BETTER CHANCE THAN EIGHT-MONTH BABIES?

There is no truth in the old wives' tale that seven-month babies are more likely to live than eight-month babies. The longer the baby stays in the uterus—until it is time for him to be born—the better chance he has for life and health. A seven-month baby may live if he has special premature care in an incubator, but an eight-month baby is much more ready for life outside. He, too, needs special care, but his chances are better.

Modern medical and nursing care can often keep a premature baby alive. But how much better it is if he can live and grow in the uterus until "term." That is why it is so important for the mother to see her doctor regularly, and to report to him anything that is different or strange, especially bleeding in the last months of pregnancy. He can often help her to keep the baby for another month or two and so increase his chances for life and health.

75. WHAT KIND OF SPECIAL CARE DOES A PREMATURE BABY NEED?

Because his body functions are not completely ready for life in the outside world, a premature baby needs many kinds of help. The normal temperature of the human body is about 98.6 degrees, Fahrenheit, but the preemie's "thermostat" cannot maintain this steady, warm temperature. He quickly becomes either too cold or too hot. So he may be placed in an incubator where the temperature and humidity are just right.

Feeding, too, can be a problem because the baby may not yet have mastered the art of sucking and swallowing. Or he may be too weak to get the food he needs from breast or bottle. Often he is fed through a tube which is inserted through his mouth or nose into his stomach. The doctor may ask the mother to extract her breast milk to feed the baby. At first, he may be fed a drop at a time. When he becomes stronger, the mother may breast-feed him if she wishes.

76. WHEN THE PREMATURE BABY IS READY TO LEAVE THE HOSPITAL, CAN HIS PARENTS REALLY TAKE CARE OF HIM?

They certainly can!

Sometimes parents may feel a bit doubtful because they have seen their baby get such specialized care in the hospital. Often when the mother is ready to go home, the baby must stay behind in the premature nursery until he is able to eat well and is gaining steadily. This can be a frustrating experience for the parents who yearn to hold him, but who must gaze at him through a glass window, and observe all the special equipment around him.

Small wonder that parents hesitate and may want to wait longer when the doctor one day says, "You can take him home." But preemies who are released from the hospital are truly ready to be treated just as if they were born on time. Often, the hospital will invite the parents to come in to handle, feed, and get really ac-

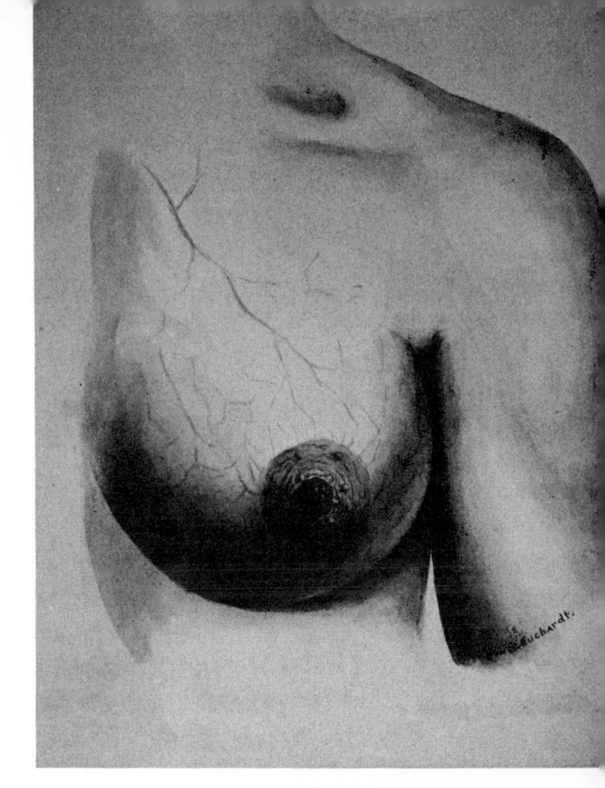

Fig. 76 In pregnancy, the blood supply in the breasts increases, the blood vessels become more visible through the skin.

quainted with their baby before he is discharged. When they finally take the baby home, they are ready.

77. WHAT ABOUT BREAST-FEEDING THE BABY?

Mother Nature provides a safe, clean, easy way to feed the baby. Women are built to do it. A woman's breasts prepare for this task during pregnancy, whether she plans to breast-feed or not. Each breast becomes fuller and tingly; and the blood supply greatly increases (Fig. 76). When the baby is born, a perfect food supply is ready. But breast milk is more than food. It also contains antibodies to build the baby's resistance to infection.

Breast-feeding brings extra dividends for the mother, too. The return of her uterus to before-pregnancy size and position is speeded up by nursing. A well-supported bosom won't lose its shape, so her figure can be as neat and trim as it was before she became pregnant.

Some mothers prefer not to nurse their babies; a few have special problems that make it difficult. Parents should talk it over together and then with the doctor before the baby comes. Fortunately, babies can thrive on formulas especially designed for them by a doctor. Remember that, breast- or bottle-fed, the baby needs love and cuddling.

For suggestions on how to get ready for breast-feeding, see page 144*ff*.

78. DOES BREAST-FEEDING HELP TO REDUCE THE MOTHER'S CHANCE OF CANCER IN LATER LIFE?

Recent medical studies indicate that mothers who breast-feed their babies have much less chance of getting breast cancer in later life. Those who have the higher risks are childless women and mothers who did not breast-feed their babies.

79. WHAT ABOUT BOTTLE-FEEDING?

Some mothers prefer to bottle-feed their babies from the start. Others may wish to breast-feed, but are told by their doctors that things would go better if the baby were bottle-fed. While this may be a disappointment, it is not a tragedy. Bottle-fed babies thrive—but they like to be held and cuddled while being fed and feeding time is a good time for communicating love to any baby.

The doctor prescribes the formula—a mixture of milk, water and sugar, or syrup—which he may change from time to time to suit the baby's growth and digestive ability.

There are three principal methods of preparing the formula: terminal sterilization, aseptic method, and tap-water method. Check with your doctor as to which method he recommends. He may even suggest using one of the ready-mixed formulas. It is good to select your pediatrician before the baby comes, so you can discuss these matters with him before the pressure is on. Then you will be ready when the baby comes home and calls for his dinner.

See page 151*ff* for the various methods of preparing the formula for bottle-feeding.

80. HOW SOON CAN MOTHERS EXPECT TO LOSE THE EXTRA WEIGHT GAINED DURING PREGNANCY?

Normally, within twenty minutes during the birth process, a mother loses nearly half the weight she gained in nine months. This includes the weight of the baby, the fluid, and the placenta. The rest of the normal pregnancy weight-gain is lost in the next few days. The uterus rapidly decreases in size, the extra volume of blood is reduced, and extra water in the tissues is excreted.

To be more specific: If you weighed 100 pounds before pregnancy, you may gain about twenty pounds. So at the end of the nine months, you weigh 120 pounds. Within a few weeks of the birth of your baby, you lose twenty pounds—most of it in a few hours—or one-sixth of your body weight! Under any other circumstances, this would be a shock. But nature is marvelous. You scarcely notice this rapid change. You just know that you feel slimmer and like your old self again.

But if you eat too much during pregnancy, you will gain extra weight. The fat gained by overeating will not be lost after the baby is born. You'll have to work to take that off.

Advance Preparation for Baby's Homecoming

81. WHAT TO BUY FOR BABY'S CLOTHING?

You don't have to spend a fortune on your baby's clothes. He outgrows them so quickly. They can be few and sensible—and appealing, too. Allow for growth, and choose items that are easy to wash and keep clean. Soft, porous, lightweight materials that are warm and durable will serve best. They should be easy to put on and take off and not interfere with free activity.

SHIRTS—4 to 6, size 1, long sleeves, 10% to 25% cotton, open down the front so that they won't have to go on over the baby's head.

DIAPERS—48, soft, absorbent, free of nap, easy to wash and dry, durable, inexpensive. Any bleached cotton material which meets these standards will serve the purpose well. (You may prefer to use a diaper service. If so, order ninety to 100 a week, and buy only a dozen of your own.)

WATERPROOF PANTS—Use discreetly because they can prevent evaporation of body moisture and cause overheating and discomfort.

NIGHTGOWNS—4 to 6, open down the front or back, easy to get baby in and out, preferably ones requiring no ironing.

SACQUES—to take the place of long nightgowns.

SWEATERS—Cardigan.

WARM WRAP: SHAWL BLANKET or BABY BUNTING—for cool days.

PARTY CLOTHES—to suit your taste. Fun, but not necessary.

82. WHAT ABOUT SUPPLIES AND OTHER EQUIPMENT FOR THE BABY?

The nursery is a very important place. Plan it carefully. You may not be able to provide a frilly, fairy-tale nursery in a tiny city apartment, but you can fix up quite comfortable quarters for the baby in a corner of one room. Choose a bright and cheerful place, out of any draft.

Keep baby's clothes and the things he needs every day in one place to save yourself unnecessary steps.

A list of the basic things you will need to equip baby's nursery follows:

FOR HIS ROOM OR CORNER

Chest of drawers

Comfortable chair for mother

Diaper pail—rust-proof (unnecessary if you use a diaper service.)

FOR HIS BED

Bassinet, basket or *crib*

Mattress—firm and waterproof

Sheets—three to six contour (You may use diapers or pillowcase in bassinet.)

Waterproof sheets —two large (You may use plastic pillowcase in bassinet.)

Waterproof pads—four to six (15″ x 20″)

Crib blankets—three

Receiving blankets—three to six, cotton flannel, for wrapping around baby

FOR HIS OUTINGS

Carriage—firm mattress
Carriage pillow (optional)
Carriage blanket
Auto bed or *seat* (with safety strap)
Diaper bag

When buying a baby carriage or other baby equipment, choose for your comfort as well as for your baby's. The handle of the baby carriage should be of such height that you can reach it with no strain on arms and shoulders. You should be able to see over the carriage hood without stretching (see Fig. 52).

The surface for bathing or changing the baby should be at hip level (see Fig. 51). For his bathing equipment, see the section on bathing the baby on page 158.

For formula-making equipment, see the section on preparing the formula for bottle-feeding on page 151*ff*.

83. SHOULD THE BABY SLEEP IN A ROOM BY HIMSELF?

Most parents like to have the new baby near them in their own room. But as the baby gets older, he may be disturbed if he sleeps in your room at night, and you may find that you are more wakeful.

By the time the baby is six months old, he should sleep in another room if it is possible. If you can't have a special nursery for the baby, make an attractive corner, but at night move his bed into the hall or the next room. Be sure of good ventilation and keep the baby out of cross-drafts.

84. WHAT KIND OF HELP DOES THE MOTHER NEED WHEN SHE GOES HOME?

One thing is certain—a new mother needs help to regain her strength. She needs a helper—husband, mother, or other relative, or a homemaker who is specially trained to help at just such a time as this. Ask the local visiting nurse association, health department, or state employment service about how and where to get a homemaker. The costs are usually geared to family income.

What kind of person should this helper be, and what should she do? She should be energetic, kind, able to follow instructions, and emotionally mature. She should be willing to help in any and all ways as the need arises: screening phone calls and visitors; preparing attractive, nutritious meals and snacks. The new mother can then spend her time resting, reading, sending out birth announcements, caring for the baby, and doing whatever exercises the doctor thinks advisable.

A homemaker (relative or professional) should be responsible for washing and ironing, cooking and cleaning. Let her tend the baby as an extra privilege. Don't let the helper care for the baby while you do the other chores—that is no rest!

If you are going to have a professional homemaker, write out what you want your helper to do—before the baby comes. Make sure she understands. This means having an interview and, if possible, a short time of trial to see if she fits in with your needs and personality.

At Home

85. WHAT ABOUT GETTING BACK INTO THE HOUSEWORK ROUTINE?

You are home from the hospital. As you begin to feel

stronger, take over the responsibilities slowly. Do what you like to do best at first, and let Grandma or Aunt Jennie or the homemaker do the rest. Don't let your helper go until you feel completely rested.

Fatigue is your worst enemy at this time. If you are too tired, you won't enjoy your baby or your family. After the helper has left, take a catnap every morning and afternoon. And be sure that you are eating well. Nothing causes fatigue more quickly than too little fuel.

You have a new and urgent responsibility in the baby—demands you never had before—along with the joys of parenthood! This time of helpless infancy is so short. Don't miss the chance to watch and enjoy your baby develop day by day—almost hour by hour! But remember, if you have other children, they need you, too.

As to housework: learn to relax and take it easy. The dusting can wait; so can the dishes in the sink. There are many short cuts to cooking—what with frozen foods and canned foods and store-bought desserts. It may cost a little more, but the health and happiness of the family are worth it.

Plan, if you can, to send out the bulk of the laundry for three or four weeks. Diaper service can relieve you of much drudgery. Perhaps grandparents or Cousin Sue can be persuaded that providing a month or two of diaper service as a gift to the baby is better than an expensive baby carriage.

If you must do some of the laundry, do a little each day instead of large wash loads twice a week. Spread out the ironing. Ask yourself: Do the sheets or Dad's B.V.D.'s have to be ironed?

86. IS THERE A BEST METHOD OF BATHING THE BABY?

Bathing the baby can be a "fun time" for all of you. You can express love by touching, holding and cuddling the baby. This is one language he understands, and he gradually responds with gurgles and kicks of joy.

There was a time when bathing the baby was a ritual. Rules were laid down, and babies were bathed "according to Hoyle" or else! New mothers went into tizzies, afraid that they might break the rules and hurt the baby.

"Oh, dear, I'm five minutes late with the bath!"

"Am I *really* holding the baby right?"

"I'm so upset. I *must* buy a white enamel tub, but I can't find one in the stores."

"I'm not comfortable bathing the baby while sitting down—but 'they' say I must!"

These perplexing days are gone, we hope, forever. What is a bath for, anyway? Is it such a big deal? Is it really necessary every day? In answer to these questions, think of yourself. Are there times when a bath is a nuisance? Have you ever skipped a bath? Did you find that it harmed you? A bath usually makes a baby feel clean and cosy, just as it does you. But there may be some days when he doesn't want to be bothered and he screams. Give him a quick once-over with a cotton ball dipped in lotion, and call it a day.

Bathe him *when* it suits you, and *how* it suits you. It really doesn't matter whether the tub is plastic or enamel; whether you stand or sit. The important questions are: Are you and the baby comfortable and relaxed about it? Is the equipment safe?

Babies used to be bathed with soap and water as soon as they were born. But it has been found that it is better to postpone bathing until the navel is healed. This means that you are likely to be the one to give the baby his first soap-and-water tub bath, because today mothers tend to leave the hospital before babies are ready for bathing.

For suggestions on one method of baby-bathing, see page 158*ff*.

87. WHY DO BABIES CRY, AND WHAT CAN YOU DO ABOUT IT?

All babies cry. Sometimes the baby cries as a form of exercise, or sometimes just to let off steam, but usually the baby is trying to tell you something. He may be wet or soiled, he may be hungry, he may be lonely and want company. A pin may be sticking him. He may have colic—gas in his stomach or intestines—and need bubbling. He may be too cold or too hot. He may simply feel out of sorts.

Dr. T. Berry Brazleton, a pediatrician of Cambridge, Massachusetts, studied eighty normal babies and found that most cried about two-and-a-half hours a day for the first seven weeks. Fussy periods, he found, tend to be concentrated between six and eleven o'clock in the evening. He thinks that this is the time when tensions mount in the family. Father comes home tired from work. He may be a bit grumpy until he gets his dinner and is settled down for the evening. Mother may be tired, too. The other children are at their most demanding. Dr. Brazleton adds that, to the naturally fatigued mother, the baby's crying is the most difficult to stand at this time of day.

Wise parents let baby have his say from six to eleven P.M., hoping that he will sleep all night.

After six weeks, the baby learns that there are other

ways to communicate with people and discharge tension—such as rolling over, watching his hands or other objects, and sucking.

When the baby cries, don't think that you have to rush to his immediate aid. On the other side of the coin, there is a big difference between letting the baby cry a few minutes and letting him cry and cry and cry. Don't let the baby's crying make you feel that you are not a good parent. Make sure that his needs are met, and then remember that *a certain amount of crying is necessary for the baby's physical development and his communication with you.*

88. HOW MUCH DO NEWBORN BABIES SLEEP?

This is a difficult question to answer because just as different adults need different amounts of sleep, so do different babies. The important things are to make sure that the baby is getting enough food, is not too hot or too cold, and is not wet or soiled. In a word—if he is comfortable, he will sleep enough to meet his growing needs. Most newborn babies will sleep until they get hungry, and when fed, burped and changed, will go back to sleep quickly. But this is not always so. Your baby may be different—and there is nothing you can do about it, and no need to worry.

A few weeks after birth, the baby usually is awake more often and for longer periods of time. As he grows older, these wakeful times increase. By the time he is one year old, he may be taking just one nap a day, usually after lunch. But again, some children need much more sleep and may continue to up until the time they go to school.

89. WHAT IS COLIC—AND WHAT TO DO ABOUT IT?

A baby with colic is uncomfortable. He has pains in his intestines. His abdomen is swelled up with gas. He pulls up his legs and screams. Just what causes colic is not fully known. The baby may be tense and easily disturbed by noise or family excitement. He may not have been burped enough after eating. He may gulp his food greedily, taking down mouthfuls of air.

Parents often become upset and occasionally angry at a persistently colicky baby. Is there something wrong with the breast milk? Or the formula? Yet often a colicky baby gains weight, perhaps more than average, and seems to be thriving in every way.

Of course, every effort should be made to quiet the baby: a little extra loving; reduction of noise and excitement, etc. Parents, especially new parents, should recognize that their uneasiness about baby care may be passed on to the baby. That is one good reason to go to expectant parents' classes to learn how to care for the baby with confidence and assurance. But if everything is done to make the baby comfortable, and he still cries, don't be disturbed. Remember that colicky babies usually get over this problem in a few months.

90. HOW TO CHOOSE A DOCTOR FOR THE BABY?

If your family doctor has watched over you during pregnancy and has helped you to have the baby, he may continue to care for both you and the baby as well as the rest of the family.

In all big cities and in some country districts, many mothers may go to hospital maternity clinics which, when the baby comes, refer them to well-baby stations, usually conducted by the health department. Or they may take the baby to a children's (pediatric) clinic in a hospital for regular examinations; for inoculations or "shots" against diphtheria, polio, measles, whooping cough, etc.; and for other care that is so important to his present and future health.

Other mothers may select a specialist (obstetrician) for their maternity care. Then, during the later months of pregnancy, they choose a pediatrician who will care for the baby as soon as he is born, helping the mother with many practical suggestions which smooth over the rough moments in the baby's early life. The pediatrician will also provide all the inoculations the baby needs, and care for him when he is sick.

The important point is to make sure that, from the moment of his birth, the baby is under the watchful eye of a doctor trained in baby care. Your obstetrician, local medical society, health department, or visiting nurse association can help you to find a baby doctor or child health service to fit your needs and your pocketbook.

91. WHEN WILL THE MENSTRUAL PERIODS RETURN?

The chances are that mothers who nurse their babies will not begin to menstruate again for about six months, or even until the baby is weaned. But this is an individual matter, and some women may begin to menstruate within four to eight weeks after delivery even though they nurse their babies.

For mothers who bottle-feed, the average date for return of the monthly periods is four to eight weeks after the baby is born. But again, some mothers may not begin menstruating for three or four months.

In the first menstrual period after the baby comes, the flow may be heavy and clotted. Sometimes the periods are irregular for a few months.

92. WHAT ABOUT SEXUAL RELATIONS AFTER THE BABY COMES?

A husband and wife should wait for a time (perhaps four weeks) after the baby comes before resuming their sexual relations. This is the reason: the stretching of the birth canal may have weakened the membranes lining the birth canal. During birth, too, the doctor may have made an episiotomy, a cut at the entrance of the vagina to give the baby more "head room" to be born. Time is needed for healing.

When intercourse is begun again, *easy does it* until about the middle of the second month after the baby is born.

V

"Baby Makes Three"— or Four or More!

93. DOES THE COMING OF THE BABY CHANGE THE FEELINGS THAT HUSBANDS AND WIVES HAVE FOR EACH OTHER?

Baby makes three is an old saying with much truth in it. Before the first baby comes, a husband and wife have a one-to-one relationship. After the baby is here, these relations change. A wife now becomes a mother of a child who demands much of her time and energy. A husband becomes a father of a family, with long-term responsibilities.

The husband of one couple recently said, "Even on

our modest income, we lived pretty well before the baby came. When I came home from the office, Ellen was at the door to meet me, relaxed and usually in high spirits. We'd talk and, perhaps, go out to some little restaurant. Evenings and weekends we saw friends, and there was time in those days for concerts, plays, and weekends in the country."

"But that was *before,*" added the wife a little ruefully. "Sometimes I meet Pete at the door with my hair a mess and still wearing a housecoat. . . . All too often Pete comes home and finds dinner behind schedule, and I've had to send him chasing off for coffee or something else we need. And the baby seems to have an intuition of his own. Just let Pete and me pick up our forks at dinner and he starts screaming. There are times, I confess, when I start screaming, too!"

Most husbands and wives who love each other adjust to these changes and are pleased with and proud of their new baby. But most couples also admit that the changes do put a strain on their marriage. It is good to know this in advance.

If the months of pregnancy and early weeks of life with baby fill you with a strange mixture of bliss and doubt, remember this is the usual state of new parents. Don't be upset, but talk over your questions *together.*

94. DO ALL MOTHERS LOVE THEIR BABIES RIGHT AWAY?

Many women believe that they should be engulfed by maternal feelings when the baby is put in their arms. Some mothers do feel warmly toward the baby from the first moment. But many a mother does not have this warm feeling toward her new baby at the start. It often takes time for a mother and baby to get acquainted. Doing for the baby, seeing his enjoyment in the bath, nursing him, feeling his tiny body—all those do wonders to develop that feeling of mother-love.

Then again, some mothers picture the baby as a real person as soon as they feel life. They think of the baby as a boy or a girl, and give him a name. They may exclaim, "Now he is excited!" or "Now he is going to sleep!" They often pat or stroke the baby through the wall of the abdomen. It is possible that these mothers can become too *tied up* with the baby and even regret the moment when the umbilical cord is cut. A mother who develops these feelings may have difficulty in adjusting to every new step in the baby's development because she feels it means further separation from her: weaning time; when the baby first says *no;* when the baby is no longer carried but steps out for himself; and so on, until adulthood. There is a great difference between mothering and smothering, and it may begin in the months *before* the baby comes or in the mother's experiences with her own mother.

Sometimes a mother does not develop a feeling for the baby during pregnancy. She will say that "it is a little organism." She knows how big it is every month and what it is like; but it is factual knowledge, not a feeling from the heart. After the baby comes, this mother, too, usually develops maternal feelings.

95. DO FATHERS USUALLY FEEL DIFFERENTLY FROM MOTHERS ABOUT THE NEW BABY?

Expectant fathers often do not have fatherly feelings in a sudden sweep of emotion. A father may daydream

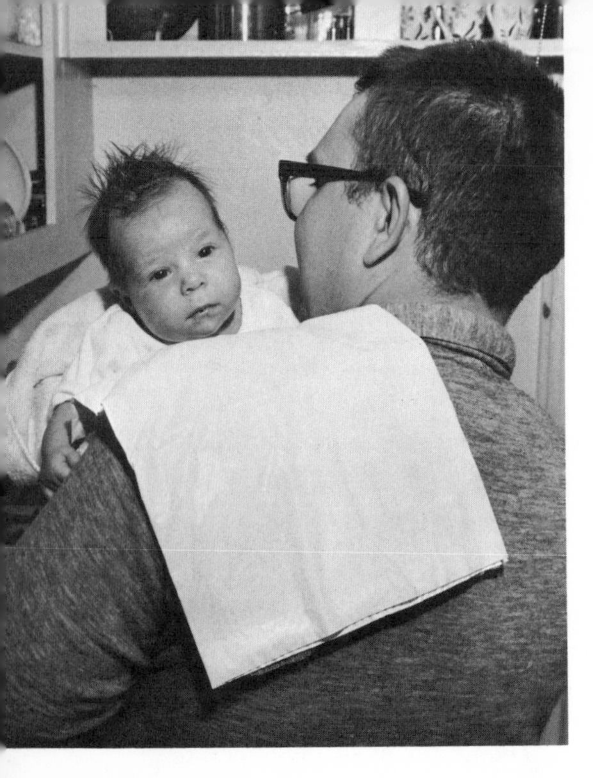

Fig. 77A Father gets acquainted by caring for the baby.

Fig. 77B Father holds his freshly bathed baby.

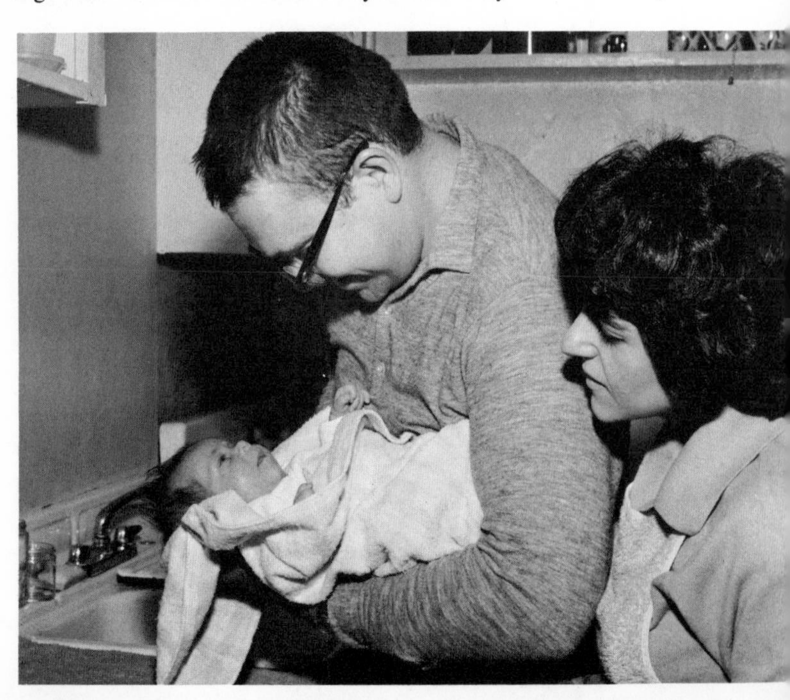

about the coming baby differently from his wife. He may completely skip the early days of infancy, imagining the time when he can take his son bowling, fishing, or to a football game. When the baby comes, he may be proud, passing out cigars and bragging a bit, but he may be inwardly disappointed with this helpless little thing in his arms (Figs. 77 A & B).

As the baby demands more of the mother's time, the father may indeed find that he is becoming jealous, but a sense of humor and an understanding point of view pave the way for happy family relations.

96. HOW SHOULD GRANDPARENTS FIT INTO THE FAMILY WITH A NEW BABY?

Grandparents and other close relatives are very important. In former days, families lived close to each other with built-in baby-sitters and close emotional ties. Grandma's lap was often a warm and comforting place for hurt feelings and bumped bodies. The viewpoint of the older generation was eagerly listened to. Today, families are often widely separated. It is not unusual for grandparents in New Jersey to have a married daughter in Illinois, another in California, and a son in Texas.

In addition, many young families live in new real-estate developments with new houses, new schools, new churches and shopping centers—and no roots! Everybody is about the same age. Everybody has the same family problems at the same time. Every other woman is pregnant or looking for a baby-sitter. This can cause young parents to feel very much alone. They really miss the viewpoint of the older generation, and the children grow up without close contact with people of more years and wider life experience than their parents.

Many families keep in contact by telephone and letter, but this does not take the place of personal relationships. Whenever grandparents can come to stay for a time, a place should be made for them. And at moments of family crisis, such as the coming of a baby, Grandma can be more valuable than rubies!

There is also the other side of this coin. Many widows live with their married children in small houses or apartments. This may be fine for the young mother (especially if it is *her* mother). But it may cause difficulties if a young married woman still relies too much on her mother. If she accepts Mother's advice in preference to her husband's, this often causes a new father to be resentful. He does not like being cut out of decision-making in the home. Grandma must come to recognize that her help, which is often badly needed, must be tempered with wisdom and moderation. Young parents, on the other hand, can accept her help, willingly given; listen to her advice; and then make up their minds independently and *together*.

Sometimes an expectant mother carries over a teenage resentment against her mother. This may cause some feelings of guilt and inward upset. But this attitude often softens during pregnancy.

97. WHAT IS THE NEW BABY'S PLACE IN THE FAMILY?

Family bickering, and the emotional upset that goes with it, can affect the baby in the uterus. It can also make it difficult for a mother to breast-feed her baby. The let-down reflex (see page 149) does not occur easily if a mother is tense and disturbed.

Often a mother suddenly recognizes that she is "trapped in the house with the baby." She may feel guilty because she is unhappy taking care of her baby instead of having the traditional feelings of mother-love. To overcome this burden of guilt, she may set about proving to herself and others that she is a good mother. She does not leave the baby for an instant, not even with a competent baby-sitter. Her husband becomes restless and irritated. Such a mother creates for herself a state of solitary confinement. No wonder she feels depressed and unhappy.

A wise mother decides at the beginning that the baby is a member of the family, and as such must fit into the family's living habits. After the rest period following the baby's birth, she takes up her usual activities at home, resumes her social contacts, goes out visiting and to community affairs with her husband and friends. Competent baby-sitters can be found in every community—if not Grandma or Aunt Suzie, then some other mother in town, perhaps a member of a baby-sitting co-operative, or a paid baby-sitter. This is important to every woman's happiness and self-respect.

Then there are times when the baby can be left with father. He may enjoy caring for the baby and being responsible for him. Diaper changing, feeding, bathing, pushing the baby carriage in the sunshine, meeting the neighbors and showing him off—all this helps a new father to get to know his baby and to recognize that the baby has a personality of his own even if he is so tiny and helpless. You can count on it: he'll be pleased when the baby first smiles at him and shows that he likes to be with father.

To put it in a nutshell: the coming of a baby tests the strength of a family, the maturity of the parents, their love for each other, their ability to get along together.

The coming of a baby is a family affair and everybody in the family is involved in it. This includes mother, father, grandparents, any other children, cousins, uncles, aunts. But more than that, a family is related to the thousands of people who have lived in the past centuries since time began and who have passed on the spark of life to this generation. The heritage of the husband's long line of ancestors joins with the heritage of the mother's ancestors to take form in the new baby. The good points of both family lines, as well as the handicaps, become intertwined in the baby's life.

What sort of person the baby will become depends not only on his inheritance, but also on how he is cared for during the months in the uterus, the earliest moments of life outside the uterus, and throughout the growing-up years.

For many parents, this is the first time that they have been entrusted *completely* with the future of another person. It is an overwhelming experience. How they accept the responsibilities of parenthood largely determines what kind of person the baby will be. What an expectant mother eats; how healthfully she lives (avoiding serious infections, unnecessary X rays, etc.); the emotional health of the family (avoiding bickering and strife)—all these and more affect the health and development of the baby. The feeling of being loved and wanted by parents who love each other is readily communicated to a tiny infant in arms. His need for affection is now recognized as an undisputed scientific fact. The care of the baby takes time and patience and plenty of hard work for both parents, but, as Kahlil Gibran has written, "Work is love made visible."

98. HOW TO DEAL WITH THE FEELINGS OF OTHER CHILDREN IN THE FAMILY?

A certain amount of jealousy is to be expected, but you can do much during the months of pregnancy to help each child feel that he is not being displaced by the new baby. Let them know about the baby's coming and the plans you are making. Let them feel the new baby moving in their mother's uterus. Help them to look forward to the baby's arrival, but at the same time make sure that they are not expecting a playmate of their own size.

If bed and rooming arrangements of any child in the family must be changed, do it *before* the baby comes. Help the youngster feel that this is a step toward being a "big" boy or girl.

When you are in the hospital, call your children on the telephone, even if they are small and can't respond. Your voice will assure and comfort them. Bring them a present when you come home from the hospital with the new baby. And, above all, be sure to set aside some time each day in which to give each one your undivided attention.

If visitors pay too much attention to the new baby, suggest that they spend a moment or two with the other children before they go.

Don't be disturbed if your youngest reverts to babyish ways for a time, or tells you that he doesn't like the baby. Don't scold him for it. Be patient and loving. In short order he will find his new place in the family.

99. IF A COUPLE HAVE QUESTIONS OR FEARS ABOUT INHERITED ABNORMALITIES THEY MAY HAND DOWN TO THEIR POSSIBLE FUTURE CHILDREN, WHERE CAN THEY GO FOR HELP?

All parents want to have healthy, normal babies. And the odds are usually in their favor. But if a baby is not normal in all respects, many handicaps can be corrected—sometimes by diet, sometimes by drugs, sometimes by surgery, sometimes by special teaching.

A handicap is often caused during pregnancy. For instance, a mother may have German measles, mumps or certain other virus diseases in the early weeks of pregnancy, perhaps even before she knows that she is pregnant. Or, in the formative weeks of the baby's life, she may unknowingly take a drug which harms the baby.

Other handicaps may be caused by inheritance. All of us carry in our genes traits for some inherited disease or condition. (Genes are the tiny bodies in ovum and sperm carrying the baby's inheritance from both family lines. See Question 5.) When we marry someone who does not have the *same* damaged genes (and the chances are excellent), the children will not be affected. Sometimes, purely by chance, husband and wife have the same damaged gene; then the baby may be affected.

Defective genes have come down through the millions of years of Man's life on this planet. Some are so numerous that all of us have the same defect but do not recognize it. Millions of years ago, for instance, Man's body manufactured its own vitamins. But this power was destroyed by defective genes. Certain diseases are caused today because people do not satisfy a specific vitamin requirement (see page 62).

Fortunately for perplexed couples, a new type of social service is developing in this country, called *heredity counseling*. An expert in genetics confers with a couple, gets all the information available on the family history of both sides. He then can tell them their chances of having a normal baby. He may say, for instance, that the odds are thirty-nine out of forty, or nineteen out of twenty. At the end of the counseling period, the couple is in a much better position to make up their minds about the problem.

Heredity counseling centers are usually affiliated with large universities. They are scattered all over the country, and the number is growing. A list of these centers may be obtained from the American Eugenics Society, 230 Park Avenue, N. Y., N. Y. 10017, for fifty cents.

100. ARE THERE OTHER HELPFUL BOOKS AND PAMPHLETS FOR PARENTS?

Yes, there are many—and here are a few:

A Baby Is Born. Maternity Center Association. New York, Grosset & Dunlap. $3.95.

Baby and Child Care. Dr. Benjamin Spock. New York, Pocket Books. 50 cents.

How to Be a Successful Mother. Eve Featheringill. New York, Wm. Morrow & Co. $3.95.

The First Nine Months of Life. Geraldine L. Flanagan. New York, Simon and Schuster. 75 cents.

The Marriage Art. Dr. John E. Eichenlaub. New York, Dell. 60 cents.

Your Child Is a Person. Dr. Stella Chess, Dr. Alexander Thomas and Dr. Herbert G. Birch. New York, Viking. $4.75.

VI

Helpful Hints

Getting Ready for Breast-feeding

However you plan to feed your baby, check your bra for fit and support. If you are planning to nurse your baby, nursing bras may be worn during pregnancy. Save expense by buying them rather than regular bras when you need a new size.

The bra should have wide straps for good uplift and alignment, supporting the breasts from below so that the nipples are held level midway between elbow and shoulder (Fig. 78). The cup of the bra should enclose the entire breast and be roomy enough to allow for future

Fig. 78 A nursing bra must provide good support. *Courtesy of* Materna

Fig. 79 The cup can be lowered. *Courtesy of* Materna

growth. A large area of the breast should be exposed when the cup is lowered (Fig. 79).

Preparing the Breasts

First wash your hands well. Clean your nails with a brush or orange stick. After your bath is often a good time for this because your hands are clean and the breasts exposed. Gently massage each breast eight to ten times, once a day. Start well above the breast and stroke with fingertips of both hands. Move downward in a firm gentle circle. Go around and then under the dark area (areola) near the nipple. Lift the breast gently and let it drop lightly. This helps to improve the circulation and to prevent engorgement which sometimes occurs on the third or fourth day after the baby

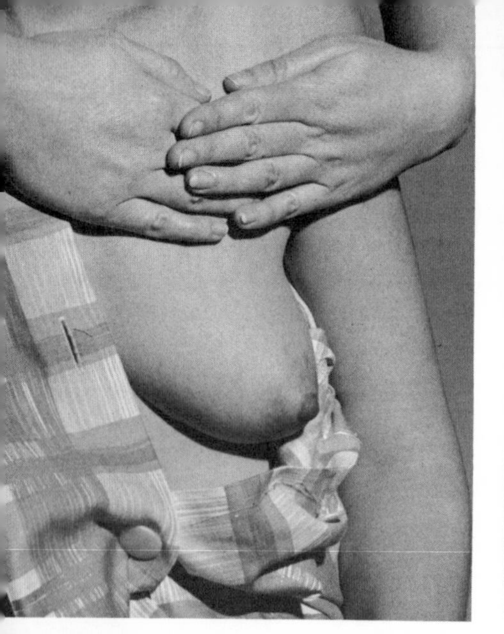

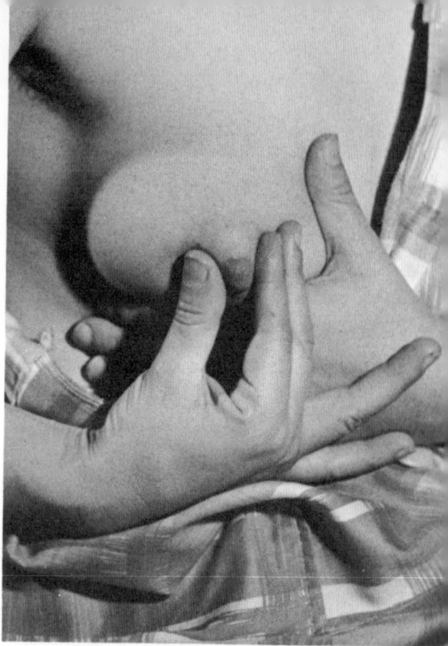

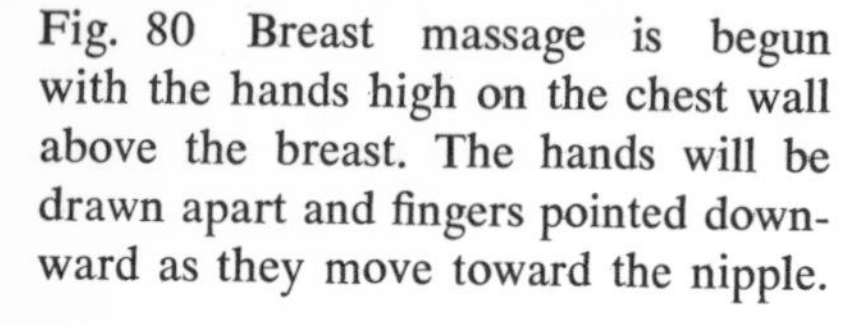

Fig. 80 Breast massage is begun with the hands high on the chest wall above the breast. The hands will be drawn apart and fingers pointed downward as they move toward the nipple.

Fig. 81 The nipple is readied for nursing by grasping it at its base with thumb and forefinger and rolling it back and forth along the index finger while exerting gentle outward pull.

is born. It is normal for the breasts to flush pink during massage (Fig. 80).

To help the nipple stand erect for nursing, press down with thumb and forefinger at the outer edge of the dark area (areola) around the nipple. Press the fingers toward each other without moving over the skin. This should cause the nipple to stand up straight. Then roll the nipple gently (Fig. 81). Support the breast with one hand, grasp the nipple at its base with the thumb and forefinger of the opposite hand. Then roll the nipple back and forth along the index finger and at the same time gently pull the nipple forward. Do this every day for a few minutes.

To keep the channels open for the later flow of milk, place your thumb and forefinger at the edge of the areola, and squeeze very gently. Then move the fingers a quarter turn and repeat the procedure. Continue around the breast every quarter turn.

When you have done this several days in a row, colostrum (a clear, milky or bright yellow sticky fluid) may appear at the nipple. Remove it with clean cotton. If colostrum or milk leaks from the nipples after the baby is born, place a clean, folded handkerchief or disposable pad inside the bra, and change it often enough to keep the nipples dry. Don't use plastic-backed pads as they prevent drying; if your bra comes equipped with these pads, remove them.

When cleaning the nipples, use a new cotton ball or pledget for each. Do not use soap on the nipple or areola because it tends to destroy the natural protective secretions. To keep the nipples soft and pliable, apply a little lubricating lotion. Rub it in well on the nipple and areola (dark area) but *not the duct opening*. Now you are ready!

Feeding the Baby

When the nurse brings your baby for his first feeding, he may hunt excitedly for your breast. Hold him gently. Don't try to force his mouth onto the nipple, but stroke his cheek nearer the nipple. He will turn toward it. Don't touch the other cheek, as he will just as quickly turn away. Lift your breast toward his searching lips. When he latches on, see that he gets his mouth well down on the dark area around the nipple, not just on the tip of the nipple.

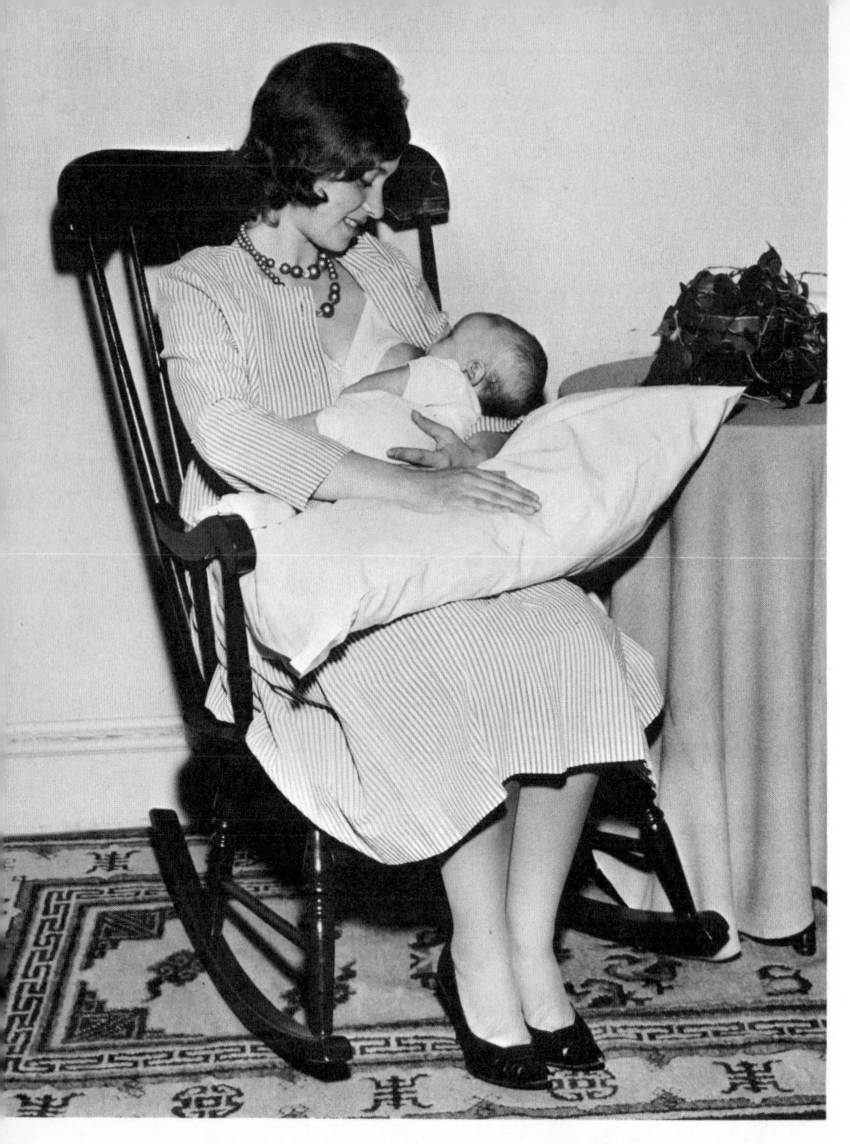

Fig. 82 When you are sitting up, select a comfortable chair which supports your back and, if possible, with arms at the right height to raise the baby to nipple level. If you wish, a low footstool may be used to support your feet. Hold the baby in a semi-sitting position on a pillow in your lap, one arm supporting his back as his head rests in the bend of your elbow.

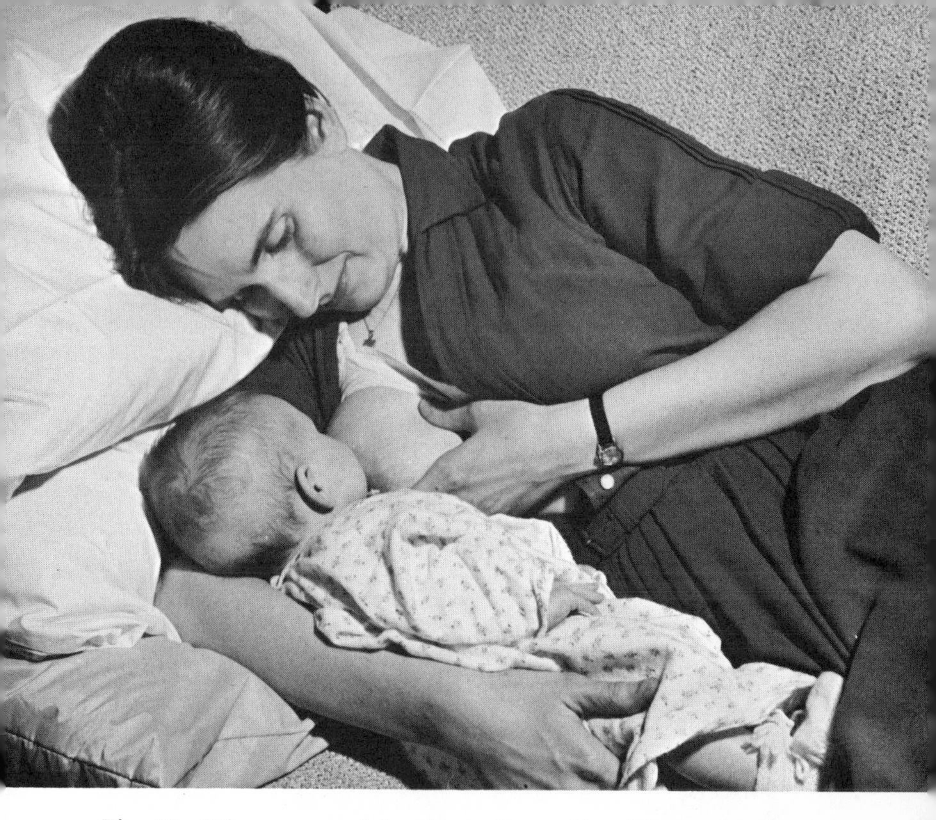

Fig. 83 When you are lying down, lie on side with your head and back comfortably supported, facing the baby. It may be necessary to rise on your arm to guide the nipple to the side of the baby's face nearest your breast. Insert the nipple into the baby's mouth so that the gums press on the areola.

Make yourself comfortable (Figs. 82 and 83). Forget the problems and chores of the day. Look at your baby. Talk to him. Cuddle him. In this state of relaxation, there is usually a gush of fluid into your breasts known as the "let-down reflex." At first the baby gets only colostrum. About the third or fourth day, the milk comes in.

Even at this early age, babies have different personalities. There are eager, greedy babies who get busy at once. There are gourmets who taste and see. There are finicky eaters. There are babies who show little interest in food. Don't become discouraged if the baby doesn't take as much as you think he should. Let the baby take what he wants, at his own speed. After a few minutes of eager nursing, he may stop. He may think he is full because an air bubble fills his stomach. Put him over your shoulder and pat his back very gently, or lay him across your knees. Take your time. Let him feel that you enjoy handling him. Be patient and you'll be rewarded.

Once he is bubbled, the baby may show interest in food again. When his rhythmical nursing gradually comes to a stop, and he falls asleep, gently put him down.

Sometimes your breasts may become hard and tender, and the baby may find it difficult to latch on to the nipple. This is a sign that you should remove some of the milk by hand. If you continue to have difficulty nursing, ask for the help of a nurse who knows about breast-feeding.

If your nipples are cracked or sore, tell your doctor. A nipple shield may be helpful. This is a rubber nipple which fits over your nipple. Be sure to wash and boil the shield between nursings.

Make sure that you are getting enough of the right foods to make your milk good and plentiful. The diet described on page 164*ff* for the second half of pregnancy should be followed, *plus* at least two more glasses of milk and another glass of orange juice a day, and a generous serving of liver at least once a week.

If you find that certain foods that you eat seem to cause discomfort in your baby, avoid them. Remember, too, that many drugs also enter the milk—aspirin, antihistamines (pills and nose drops), etc. Take only those drugs recommended by your doctor.

Will smoking hurt the baby? For sure, he certainly doesn't need it! If you must smoke, cut down on the number of cigarettes a day. Start cutting down while you are pregnant. It will make it easier.

What about drinking? A cocktail before dinner or an occasional glass of beer or wine are OK, but don't overdo. Drinks add a lot of calories to your diet!

Hospitals usually run on a fixed schedule, so your baby may be brought to you from the nursery at regular three- or four-hour intervals. You don't have to abide by the same timetable at home. Your baby may not like it, or it may not fit your own routine. Try to fit feeding times to your baby's appetite and your family's way of life. If you have your baby beside you in the hospital (rooming-in), you may get used to feeding him when he asks for it. One of the big advantages of rooming-in is that you and your baby are accustomed to each other before you go home from the hospital.

Take care of your breasts to avoid infection and discomfort. After nursing, dry your nipples gently. Some mothers say that leaving them exposed to the air for five to ten minutes keeps the skin healthy.

Preparing the Equipment and Formula for Bottle-feeding

There are several methods of preparing the equipment and formula for bottle-feeding: terminal sterilization; the aseptic method; the tap-water method; and the easiest (and most expensive) of all, the ready-packs.

Your doctor will give you the formula he wants you to use, including the amount of each ingredient.

Terminal Sterilization and Aseptic Methods

If you use either of these methods, you will need the following equipment:

bottles: 12 eight-ounce for milk
2 four-ounce for water or orange juice

nipples: enough so you will have to boil them only once a day—one for each feeding and each drink of water or orange juice.
The holes in the nipples may need to be made larger. To test, put milk in a bottle, put on the nipple, and squeeze. The milk should come out one drop at a time.
To make the holes larger, heat a small needle in the flame of a match until red-hot. Push the hot needle through the hole in the nipple. Don't use too large a needle because the hole may then let the milk come out too fast, causing the baby to choke.

nip-caps: covers for nipples, made of aluminum, glass, or plastic—enough for the day's supply of formula bottles.

kettle with tight-fitting lid and removable rack: large enough to hold the day's bottles and other equipment. If you have a large kettle, make a substitute rack by putting a perforated pie tin or a folded cloth in the bottom.

bottle brush: long-handled brush with stiff bristles to scrub bottles. Bend tip so bristles reach into every corner of bottle.

measuring cup—marked in ounces

set of measuring spoons

long-handled spoon

funnel

tongs

saucepan: two-quart capacity

jar with perforated top if using *terminal sterilization method.* (In terminal sterilization, the formula is put into bottles cold, and then the bottles—nipples and all—are sterilized together.)
or

small saucepan to boil nipples in, if using the *aseptic method.* (In the aseptic method, the formula is boiled separately and then put into bottles which have also been boiled.)

Preparation
Both Methods

1. Wash your hands well.
2. Wash all equipment with hot water and soap.
3. Clean inside of bottles, nipples, and nipple covers with brush.
4. Force water through nipple holes. If clogged, clean with toothpick.
5. Rinse everything in clean hot water, and drain.

Terminal Sterilization

6. Measure milk, water and sugar or syrup into saucepan.

7. Mix enough for 24 hours. If you use evaporated milk, wash top of can with soap and water, and rinse before opening can. If you use whole milk, shake well to mix in the cream.

8. Pour formula into bottles through funnel.

9. Put nipples on bottles. (Put covers on loosely.)

10. Stand bottles upright in kettle on wire rack.

11. Add water to kettle until it reaches level of milk in bottles.

12. Cover with tight-fitting lid.

13. Bring to a boil.

14. Boil for 25 minutes by the clock.

15. Tighten covers over nipples when bottles are cool enough to touch.

16. Put bottles in refrigerator.

17. Serve warm or cold (ask your doctor) when "ordered."

Aseptic Method

6. Put bottles upside down in rack in kettle.

7. Put funnel, tongs, spoons in kettle.

8. Put nipples into a clean jar with perforated lid.

9. Put nipple jar in kettle upside down. Boil 5 minutes by the clock. (You may boil nipples separately in small saucepan with tight-fitting lid.)

10. Pour about 2 inches of water into bottom of kettle.

11. Put on tight-fitting cover.

12. Bring to a boil.

13. Boil for 5 minutes by the clock.

14. Leave everything in kettle to cool and ready for use.

15. Measure milk, water and sugar or syrup into large saucepan.

16. Add ounce or so of water beyond what the formula calls for. This allows for evaporation.

17. Mix enough for 24 hours. If you use evaporated milk, wash top of

Aseptic Method

can with soap and water, and rinse, before opening can. Shake whole milk well.

18. Boil formula for 3 to 5 minutes, stirring constantly.
19. Take from fire, but continue to stir to cool it and keep scum, which clogs nipples, from forming.
20. Take bottles from kettle with tongs. Don't touch tops.
21. Pick up funnel, not touching rim or inside.
22. Pour formula into bottles.
23. Put boiled nipples on bottles without touching rim or top of nipples. (This takes practice!)
24. Cover nipples with caps.
25. Put in refrigerator.
26. Serve warm or cold (ask your doctor) when "ordered."

Tap-water Method

Some pediatricians recommend the tap-water method.

The formula is made up each time the baby is fed, so fewer utensils are needed: just a few bottles and nipples, nip-caps, measuring cup, bottle brush, long-handled spoon, and a saucepan in which to boil this equipment.

For the tap-water method, the water quality must be excellent. If not, the water must be boiled three minutes and cooled before the formula is made.

1. Wash bottles and utensils in hot soapy water, rinsing in clean hot water.
2. Wash and boil nipples for 5 minutes just before use.
3. Prepare the formula just before the baby is fed.
4. Measure the correct amount of sugar or syrup into a clean dry bottle.
5. Add the right amount of hot tap water, making sure all is dissolved.
6. Add evaporated milk to the mixture. Before opening a new can of milk, wash and rinse the top thoroughly.
7. Put on the nipple—and the formula is ready.

If the baby does not take all of the formula, throw out what is left. After the feeding, rinse the bottle, nipple and cap in clean cold water. Then scrub with brush in hot soapy water. Rinse thoroughly in hot tap water. The bottle should be boiled for five minutes or washed in an automatic dishwasher at least once a day.

Ready-packs

If all this seems to be too much trouble, you can buy packs of ready-mixed and sterilized formula at your pharmacy. This will keep without refrigeration. Just stack the formula on the shelf and, when it's feeding time, remove the top and feed the baby. Then throw the bottle away. This is much more expensive than home-prepared formula, but it is easier and quicker. However, you must *make sure that the ready-made formula has your doctor's approval.*

Feeding the Baby

There is no one ideal position for feeding. Each mother finds the most comfortable position for herself and her own baby. Many select a chair that supports the back (often a rocking chair), with arms at the right height to support the baby without strain. Feet may be flat on the floor or on a footstool, or perhaps one foot on the floor, the other on the footstool. Sometimes it helps to hold the baby in a semi-sitting position on a pillow as shown in Figure 84.

Fig. 84 A comfortable position for bottle-feeding the baby.

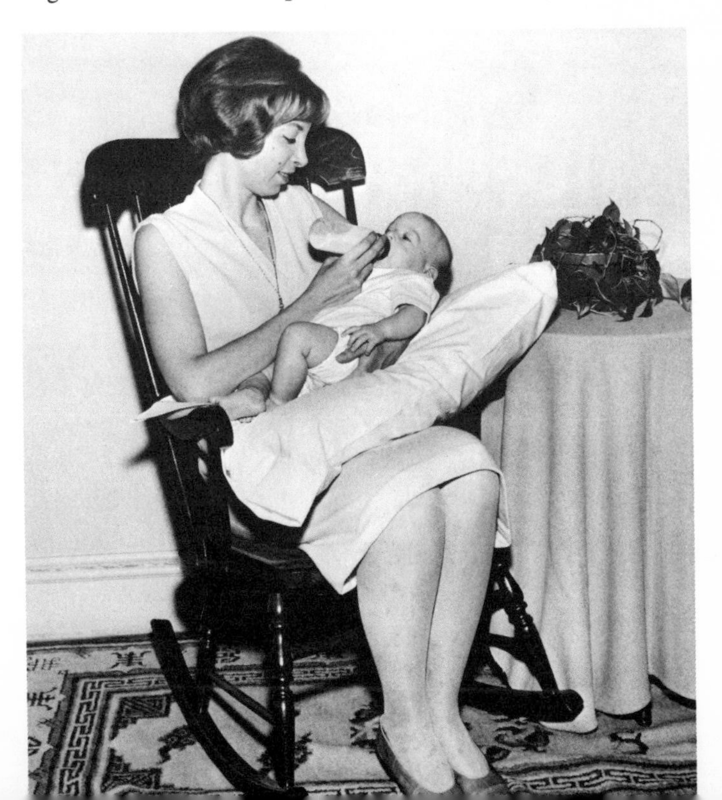

Bathing the Baby

Bath Equipment for the Carriage Set

Bath equipment can be simple and inexpensive. You need:

Long apron (to protect yourself from splashes!)

Washcloths —2-4

Bath towels—2-4

Tub (plastic or metal): A big dishpan will do but, if you like the expensive baby bathtubs, by all means get one to suit your fancy.

Dressing table with top high enough so you won't have to bend when you are caring for the baby.

Toilet tray: 1 covered jar for cotton balls or tufts. You may prefer a cotton "picker."

1 covered jar for safety pins
1 covered soap container for mild soap
1 container baby oil, lotion or cream (take your choice), or powder

One Method of Baby-bathing

The art of baby-bathing is simple and easy. Here is just one method:

1. Set the time so the baby won't get impatient and hungry before the bath is over. You don't want him to associate his hunger pangs with bath time.
2. Put bathing equipment in a place that is warm but not hot (between 75 and 80 degrees F), and free of drafts.
3. Wash your hands.
4. Arrange everything within easy reach, including the baby's clothes (Fig. 85).

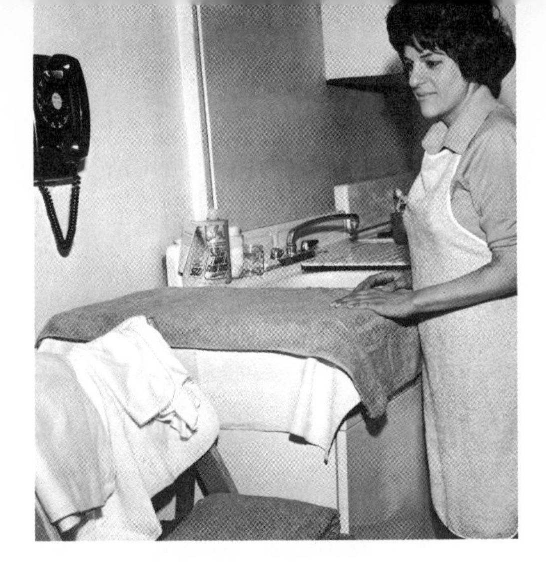

Fig. 85

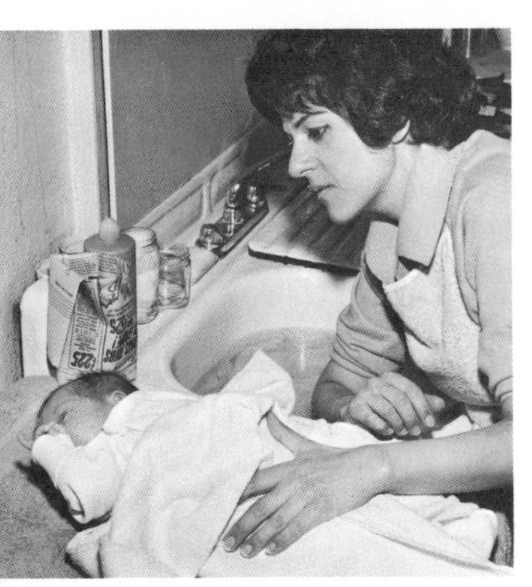

Fig. 86

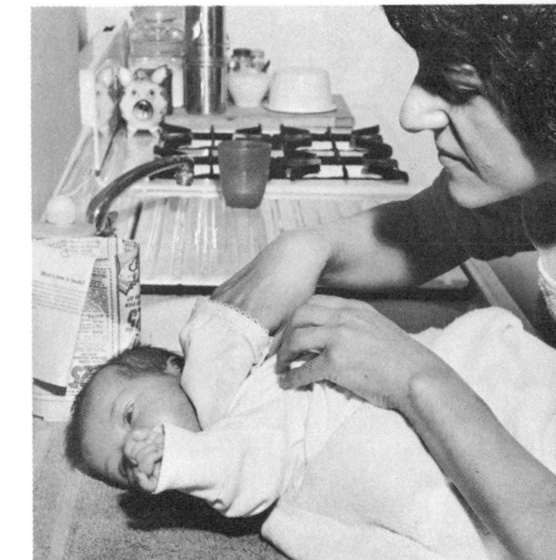

Fig. 87

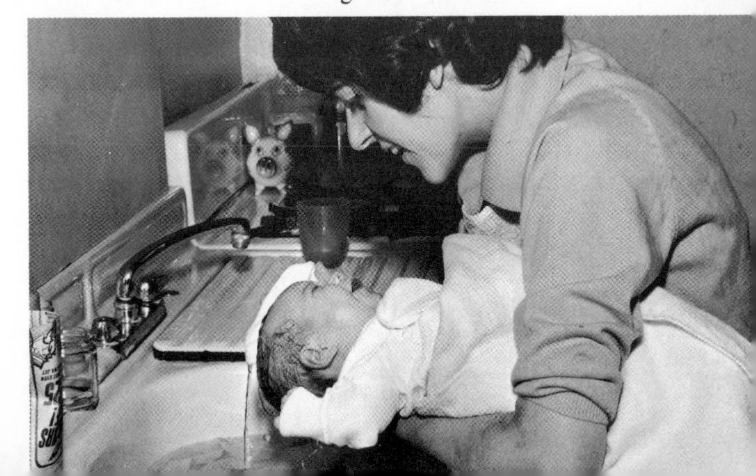

Fig. 88

5. Take the covers off the jars on the toilet tray.

6. Put an inch or two of warm water in the tub. Test it for temperature with your elbow before you put the baby in. It should feel comfortably warm (Fig. 86).

7. Put the baby on top of the dressing table, and undress him except for shirt and diaper (Fig. 87).

8. Wash his face with a wet washcloth—no soap (Fig. 88).

9. Wipe his eyes. If there is encrustation in the corners use a new cotton ball for each eye. Wipe once from inner corner of eye outward.

10. Wash around each nostril if there is any discharge, being careful not to get water up his nose.

11. Wash his ears, just the outside; don't go in deep. Wash behind his ears.

12. Make a lather in your hands with the soap, then raise the baby's head to wash his hair. Using a circular motion, gently wash his scalp starting at the hairline in front, going to the back. Keep the baby's head tilted back so the soap won't get into his eyes. Don't be afraid of the soft spot (fontanelle); it is tougher than you think. Using the football hold (with the baby tucked under your arm as a football player runs with the ball), rinse his head with the washcloth and pat dry.

13. Take off the baby's shirt and diaper (Fig. 89). Be sure to close all safety pins and put them in the pin jar.

14. Suds the baby all over, and lower him into the tub, feet first, keeping his head out of water. Hold him firmly, with the back of his head and neck resting against your left wrist and your fingers circling around his left shoulder and armpit. Support the baby's buttocks with your right hand as you grip his left thigh with thumb and forefinger (Fig. 90). If you are left-handed, reverse the position.

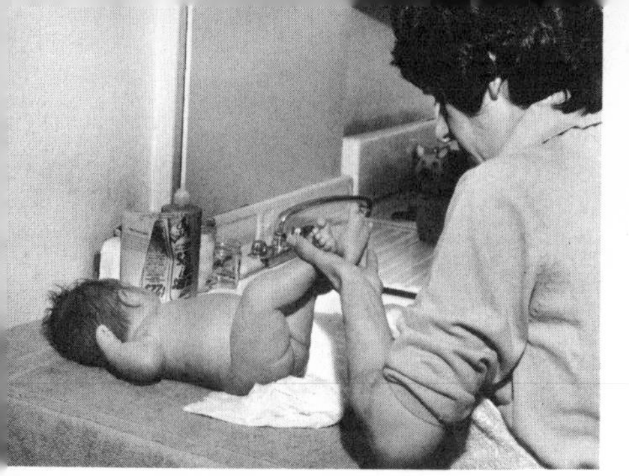

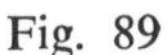

Fig. 89

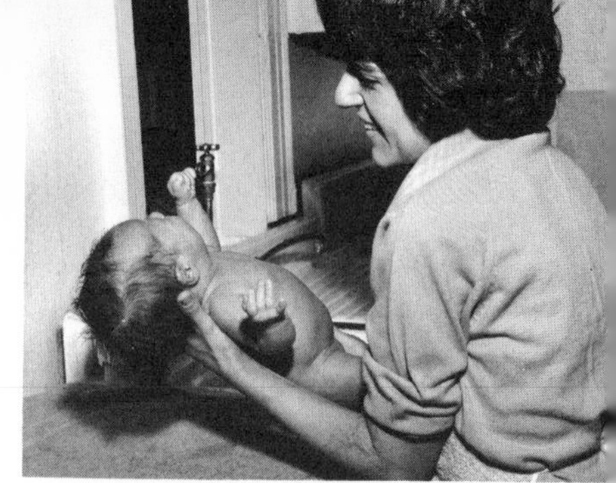

Fig. 90

15. Rinse the baby's back (Fig. 91), then reverse the hold, and rinse the front (Fig. 92). *Never turn him over.*

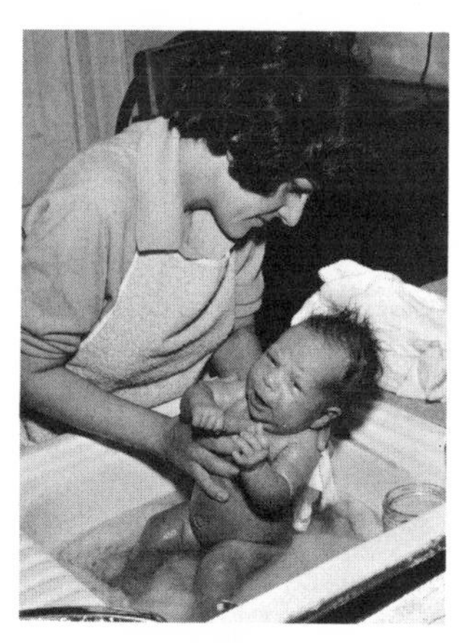

Fig. 91

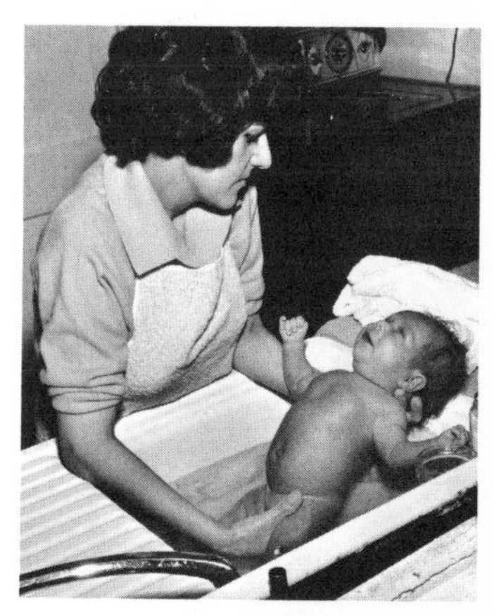

Fig. 92

16. If he wants to play, let him enjoy himself for a few minutes. This is baby's time of day when all your attention is on him. Don't let anything interrupt—the telephone or door bell or people talking to you. Talk to the baby; sing, if you like. Soon he will answer back with coos and smiles. In this way the baby learns that bath time is fun. He will kick the water and enjoy splashing you.

17. Lift the baby out of the tub—using the same grip.

18. Place him on a towel and pat him dry all over (Fig. 93), particularly in the creases and groin, behind the knees, and between the toes.

19. Powder or oil. Use one or the other, just as you would for yourself. Powder is a "dryer-upper"; oil, lotion or cream lubricates dry skin. Squeeze a drop or two of baby lotion or oil into the palm of your hand and gently rub it into any dry skin areas. If you use powder, don't shake it on him, but put a little in the palm of your hand and pat it on. It is not good for a baby to breathe in powder.

20. Dress the baby (Fig. 94).

21. Then into bed—and the trick is done (Figs. 95 A and 95 B).

Fig. 93

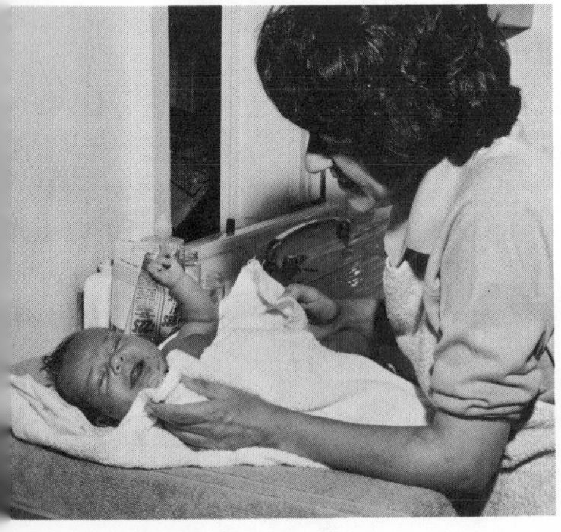

Fig. 94

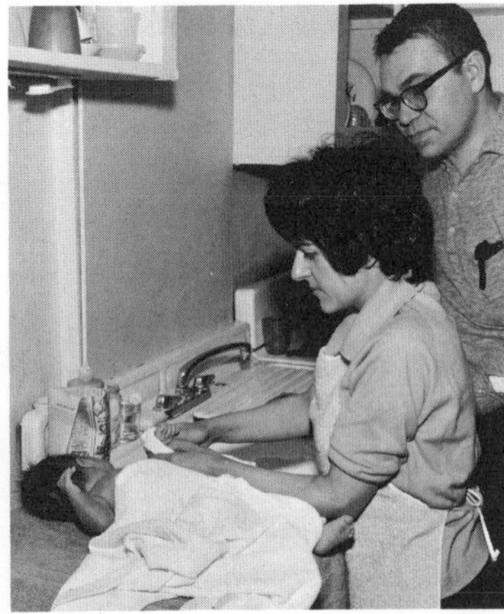

Fig. 95A Putting the baby to bed in his own crib.

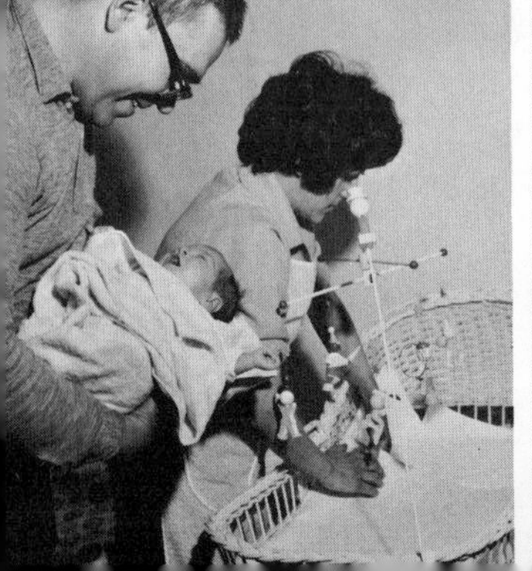

Fig. 95B

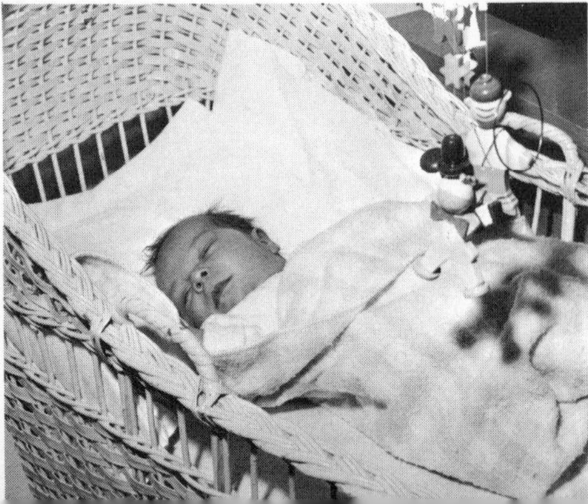

Choosing the Right Foods in Pregnancy

During the First Half of Pregnancy

2 servings (two ounces each) *every day* of
  meat or
  fish or
  poultry or
  cheese
3 to 5 eggs *every week*
2 glasses of milk *every day*
  If you have trouble drinking milk, substitute
  for each glass:
    1 slice of cheese or
    1⅓ cups of cottage cheese or
    ½ cup of evaporated milk or
    ½ cup of instant powdered milk
4 servings *every day* of
  vegetables—dark green or yellow—or
  fruits—But be sure to have at least an orange or
      ½ grapefruit or a glass of tomato juice
      every day.
4 servings *every day* of
  bread (a serving is 1 slice) or
  cereal (a serving:
    cooked cereal—½ cup
    ready-to-eat cereal—1 ounce
    cooked rice—⅓ cup
    cooked macaroni—½ cup
    cooked spaghetti—½ cup) or
  potato—1 medium

During the Second Half of Pregnancy

After the fourth month, the baby rapidly begins to increase in weight. In the last three months alone, he triples his weight. This means that the mother's food requirements become greater in order to maintain her own strength and energy and allow for the baby's growth.

3 servings (two ounces each) *every day* of
  meat or
  fish or
  poultry or
  cheese
1 egg *every day*
6 glasses of milk or milk substitutes *every day*
6 servings *every day* of
  vegetables—dark green or yellow—or
  fruits—But be sure to have an orange or grapefruit *twice a day*
4 servings *every day* of
  bread or
  cereal or
  potato

For most people, this may not be enough food to satisfy. From the above list make your own choices for extra food, perhaps increasing portions by one-third.

Choosing the Right Foods for a Low-sodium Diet

Try the following suggestions for restricted sodium diets. You *can* add flavor and appeal to nearly everything you eat. Natural seasonings such as herbs, lemon juice, onion, garlic and vinegar can really bring out natural flavors of vegetables, meats, and other foods.

If both calories and sodium are restricted on your diet, eliminate any combination suggested which contains sugar, honey, excess butter, cream, and the like.

Listed below are general suggestions to help until experience teaches you what seasonings and amounts give the most pleasing results. Use herbs sparingly until you are sure what they can do for food. If dried, add them to liquid, if possible, so flavors will blend more easily.

SOUPS:

Cook soup bones with fresh vegetables like carrots, celery, onions and tomatoes. Season with bay leaves, cloves, pepper and dill weed or dill seed.

Float thin slices of lemon on unsalted tomato bouillon. A sprig of parsley pulled through the center of the slice of lemon adds glamor and appetite appeal.

MEATS:

Lean Beef

Squeeze lemon juice on the meat, sprinkle with dry mustard and pepper.

Dust sage over the top of a roast before baking.

Cook with different vegetables.

Other suggested flavorings are marjoram, nutmeg, onion, thyme, bay leaf.

If allowed, grape jelly is good as an accompaniment.

Hamburger Patties

Season by squeezing lemon juice into the meat before cooking. Dust with paprika and pepper.

Add chopped onion or oregano.

When cooking on the charcoal grill,

	toss a few bay leaves onto the coals under the hamburgers. Other herbs may be used.
Pot Roast	A teaspoon of mixed pickling spice with a pot roast gives a delicious flavor. Add a garlic bud.
Meat Loaf	Lemon juice can be added. Poultry seasoning. Chili powder and tomato as well as onion.
Stews or Casseroles	Include such flavorings as dried chili powder, parsley, ¼ teaspoon nutmeg, ½ teaspoon ginger, small amounts of sage, basil or thyme, bay leaf and curry.
Liver	Broil, but brush with a mixture of lemon juice, unsalted butter and grated onion before turning.
Lamb	Use curry or oregano in lamb stew. Mint, garlic, rosemary, vinegar sauce with a little sugar, broiled pineapple rings.
Pork	Sprinkle with lemon juice and dust with paprika, onion, garlic, sage. Serve with applesauce, spiced apples or cranberries.
Veal	Bay leaf, ginger, marjoram, curry, dill seed or dill weed. Serve with currant jelly and spiced apricots.
POULTRY:	Stew chicken with a bay leaf, some celery leaves, onion and black pepper. Broiled chicken may be sprinkled with powdered rosemary, thyme or sage and some lemon juice.

Broiled chicken may also be basted with a sauce of lemon juice, olive or salad oil and a crushed clove or garlic bud, paprika for color.

Basil.

May be served with mushrooms or cranberry sauce.

FISH:

Rub fish inside and out with fresh lemon before cooking to add flavor.

Use plain lemon or lemon-butter mix (see recipe on page 172).

Broiled fish blends well with lemon juice, black pepper and onion.

For baking, try wrapping fish in foil with a slice of lemon, a bay leaf, pepper and a little onion. Bake until tender and serve in foil.

Other seasonings are dry mustard, paprika, tarragon, curry and mushrooms.

EGGS:

Put a teaspoon of vinegar or onion in the water for *poaching eggs.*

Eggs may be *scrambled* in unsalted fat with a pinch of mixed herbs, or with fresh tomato cut up with them or green pepper or dried chives.

Orange juice, pineapple juice or tomato juice may be used instead of milk in scrambled eggs.

Add curry, rosemary or basil to scrambled eggs.

Gingerale may be used in *omelets.*

Jelly, pineapple, and applesauce may be used in omelets.

Use a few drops of lemon juice or

	vinegar on cooked eggs.
	For *deviled eggs,* or an *egg salad mixture,* mash the yolks of hard cooked eggs or whole chopped eggs with a little milk, vinegar or lemon juice, powdered mustard, garlic, black pepper and salt-free mayonnaise.
	Other additions might be pepper, green pepper, mushrooms, dry mustard, paprika, curry.
VEGETABLES:	The general rule to use is ¼ teaspoon herb to three cups cooked vegetables. A small amount of sugar added during the cooking period helps to bring out the natural flavor of the vegetables.
Asparagus	Lemon juice.
	Sour cream.
	A few unsalted nuts might be added.
Beans, Green	Cook in a small amount of water, adding curry or basil.
	Add cream, unsalted butter and parsley.
	Unsalted slivered almonds.
	Serve with lemon juice, unsalted butter and a bit of grated onion or chopped chives.
	Cold, cooked green beans with vinegar and onion may be used as salad.
	Other seasonings are marjoram, nutmeg, unsalted French dressing, dill seed.
Broccoli	Lemon juice or onion.
Brussel Sprouts	Lemon juice with unsalted butter with a dash of dry mustard and marjoram.

	Vinegar may also be used.
Cabbage	Lemon juice or vinegar plus a dash of dry mustard and marjoram.
	Onion juice or raw onion rings.
	Mustard dressing, dill seed, unsalted butter with lemon and sugar.
Carrots	Cinnamon, nutmeg, or ginger and unsalted butter.
	Lemon butter.
	Glaze with brown sugar.
	Lemon or orange juice and parsley.
	Sprinkle with orange rind.
	Fresh mint, minced, adds color and flavor.
	Thyme, rosemary or bay leaves may also be cooked with them.
Cauliflower	Nutmeg.
	Lemon juice and unsalted butter with a dash of dry mustard and marjoram.
Corn	Green pepper, tomatoes.
Peas	Chopped or powdered mint.
	Orange rind.
	Marjoram, parsley, chives, rosemary, onion and mushrooms.
Potatoes, Baked	Lemon juice, unsalted butter and grated onion.
	Season with unsalted fat or sour cream, chives or grated onion.
Potatoes, Mashed	Nutmeg, cream, unsalted butter.
	Chopped parsley.
	Sour cream with dry horseradish or chives.
	Curry with chopped chives or parsley.
	Minced onion.

Potatoes, Boiled	Boil in jackets and season with unsalted fat, minced parsley and fresh dill or dill seed or dill weed. Mace, chopped green pepper, onion.
Squash	Frozen squash may be used. Lemon or orange juice and cinnamon. Ginger or mace. Brown sugar and molasses. Boiled Hubbard squash with sour cream and dill seed. Mash with lemon juice, unsalted butter, brown sugar and cinnamon or ginger. Black pepper.
Sweet Potatoes	Candied or glazed with cinnamon or nutmeg or cloves. Orange slices. Scalloped with apples and sugar.
Tomatoes	Basil or oregano. Sugar. Unsalted butter. Onion.
SALADS:	Marinate cucumber slices and onion rings in lemon juice or vinegar. Add sugar, if desired. Mix equal amounts of lemon juice and sugar to top a fresh tomato or other vegetable salad. Use honey mixed with lemon juice for a simple, sweet fruit salad dressing. Add orange and pineapple chunks to cabbage and mixed green salad—good with salt-free French dressing,

or salt-free mayonnaise.

Unsalted nuts add flavor and texture to fruit and vegetable salads.

Green bean salad is good with lemon juice, oil, chopped parsley and garlic or onions.

Chilled, cooked beet slices may be seasoned with vinegar and pickling spice for a relish or salad.

Minced fresh basil or the powdered herb on sliced tomatoes.

Unsalted tomato juice, heated with oregano and basil may be made into gelatin salad by using unflavored gelatin and lemon juice and perhaps grated onion.

SALAD DRESSINGS:

Mayonnaise

1 egg or 2 egg yolks
3 tablespoons lemon juice or vinegar
1 teaspoon sugar
1 teaspoon dry mustard
½ teaspoon paprika
2 cups vegetable oil

Beat egg with 1 tablespoon of the lemon juice. Add sugar, dry mustard and paprika, beating until well blended. Add oil, a little at a time, beating constantly until a thick mixture forms. As mixture thickens, oil can be added more rapidly, while beating constantly. When dressing is very thick, beat in remaining lemon juice or vinegar; then add remaining oil gradually, beating until well blended.

French Dressing

1 cup vegetable oil
½ cup lemon juice or vinegar
½ teaspoon dry mustard
½ teaspoon paprika
¼ teaspoon pepper

Combine well and keep covered in refrigerator. Shake well before using.

Zero Salad Dressing

½ cup unsalted tomato juice
2 tablespoons lemon juice or vinegar
1 tablespoon onion, finely chopped
Pepper to taste

Chopped parsley, green pepper, dry mustard or other herbs may be added also.

Combine and shake well. Store in refrigerator.

This dressing is excellent if there is a calorie restriction also.

LEMON BUTTER RECIPE:

½ cup butter (¼ pound)
2 teaspoons grated lemon rind
3 tablespoons lemon juice

Cream butter, blend in gradually lemon juice and lemon rind. Whip with the electric mixer.

Variations

⅛ teaspoon savory and ⅛ teaspoon rosemary may be added.

Chopped fresh parsley may be added for a sandwich spread or may be used for meats and vegetables.

1 tablespoon chopped fresh herbs or 1½ teaspoons approved dry herbs.

Use on meats and vegetables; vary amounts to individual taste.

1 tablespoon grated onion or chopped chives. Excellent on baked potatoes; try also on green beans and squash.

¼ teaspoon dry mustard and ¼ teaspoon marjoram are very good on steamed cabbage.

½ teaspoon nutmeg, cinnamon, or ginger is good on cooked carrots.

Mixture may be placed on waxed paper and molded into a roll and frozen. Cut off pats and use as needed.

GENERAL SUGGESTIONS:

Cooking Fats	May be selected from unsalted vegetable fats and oils such as Crisco, Spry, Wesson Oil, Mazola, unsalted lard, unsalted butter or unsalted margarine.
Removing Salt from Margarine or Butter	If unsalted butter is not available, salt may be taken from margarine or butter as follows: Boil one quart of water and ¼ pound of margarine until well melted. Mix well with fork. Let cool. When firm, remove fat from top of water. Keep covered and cold. Most of the salt is left in the water. Discard water.
Potassium Bicarbonate	Substitute in equal amounts for sodium bicarbonate in recipes which call for baking soda.
Sodium-free Baking Powder	Use in the proportion of 1½ teaspoons for each teaspoon of regular baking powder.

Recipes Without Leavening Agents	Brownies, shortbread, thin sugar cookies—make without the addition of salt.
Pies	Prepare with unsalted pie crust.
Bread	Leaven with yeast but add no salt. A sweet dough can also be made with cinnamon and sugar added.

Check all labels to see if *salt* or *sodium* are included.

In cooking for the family where one person is on a low-sodium diet, cook vegetables for all at the same time and take out the portion for the diet before adding seasoning for the family. Many of the ideas listed here may be used for the entire family.

Oil with herbs added may be used for seasoning when fat is allowed in the diet. It could be substituted for an equal amount of unsalted butter or other fat.

Vanilla or other extracts, grated lemon or orange rind, and spices may be used for seasoning.

Fruits are naturally low in sodium and may be used as your doctor advises you. Applesauce with a bit of spice added may be used as a relish with meats. Citrus fruit juices or fruits should be used daily for their vitamin value. Fruit may be substituted for desserts.

For between-meal snacks, raw vegetables or fruits may be used. Unsalted nuts may be used if your doctor approves.

Courtesy of Nutrition Section, Minnesota State Health Department

Planning Future Babies

Many husbands and wives plan their families on the basis of the wife's health; how many children they believe they can support and educate; and how many they feel prepared to love and care for.

There are many ways to control the number of children in a family. Husbands and wives can get medical advice and help in family planning at their doctor's office, hospital maternity clinic, or local Planned Parenthood center.

Here are some practical, birth-control methods:

"The Pill"

Couples who choose this method should consult their doctor immediately after their baby is born. The doctor who knows the mother's condition can tell her whether there is any reason for her not to take these pills which stop the release of eggs from the ovaries.

If the doctor gives her a prescription, the woman starts taking the pills five days after her last menstrual period began. She takes one pill each day for twenty days at about the same time of day; then stops. Within five days after the last pill is taken, menstruation will begin. Five days later, she starts taking the pills again. If this method is followed very carefully, it is nearly one hundred percent effective.

Because some women have problems when they take these pills, it is very important to keep in touch with the doctor and to report any out-of-the-ordinary symptoms.

Intrauterine Device (IUD)

The doctor places a small plastic or stainless steel spiral, loop, ring or bow (called an intrauterine device, or IUD) through the vagina into the womb or uterus. When the woman wants to have a baby, the doctor takes it out through the vagina.

When the IUD is in place, sex relations are not disturbed in any way. The woman may find that her monthly periods are heavier, however, and she may have some cramps after it is first inserted. Bleeding and spotting between periods may also occur.

Sometimes the IUD is expelled from the uterus without the woman knowing it. But, among those women who do retain it, the IUD is about ninety-seven percent effective.

Diaphragm with Contraceptive Jelly or Cream

The doctor measures the opening of the woman's birth canal and provides her with a rubber cup whose rim is a lightweight spring padded with rubber. This rubber cup fits over the mouth of the womb (cervix). Its purpose is to block the sperm from entering the uterus.

The doctor teaches the woman how to apply a sperm-killing jelly or cream to the rubber cup (called a diaphragm) and how to insert it before she has sex relations. The diaphragm must be left in place for at least six hours after intercourse. It can be worn up to twenty-four hours without harm.

This is an effective method provided the directions are followed carefully *and* the diaphragm is checked each time for tiny holes which might let the sperm pass through.

Condom

The condom (or "rubber") is placed over the man's penis after erection in the sexual act. This is a highly effective method, especially if the wife uses a contraceptive jelly, cream or foam. In addition, the husband must hold the condom tightly to the penis as he withdraws from the vagina, to prevent spilling of sperm. A new condom of a recognized brand should be used for each sex act, and the condom examined for tiny holes before use. Some couples feel that the condom interferes with full enjoyment of intercourse.

Contraceptive Foams, Creams and Jellies

There are a number of foams, creams and jellies, but most authorities agree that the foams are the most effective. They may be used without the diaphragm or condom with a reasonable chance of effectiveness.

The creams and jellies, which some consider messy, are most effective when used with a diaphragm or condom.

Foaming tablets and suppositories are considered the least effective.

Rhythm Method

For those who cannot or do not want to use any of the above methods of birth control, the rhythm method —if carefully practiced—will reduce the chances of conception.

A woman can become pregnant only at the time each month when an egg (ovum) is released from her ovary. This happens about two weeks before the beginning of the next menstrual period. The ovum, when released, may live several days. Pregnancy can occur only when sex relations take place during this critical time. If husband and wife do not have sex relations during that time, she will not become pregnant.

The chief drawback to this method is the difficulty of knowing exactly when the ovum is ready for fertilization by a sperm. The doctor studies the woman's ovulation pattern and estimates the days each month to avoid intercourse. Many women, however, are not regular, and the probable days of ovulation cannot be easily pinpointed. Among those who are usually regular, changes of climate or living habits, illness or shock may temporarily disturb the monthly periods. Because of these problems, the rhythm method is not reliable for some women.

Index

NOTE: Refer to *Contents* at beginning of book for references to information on general topics.